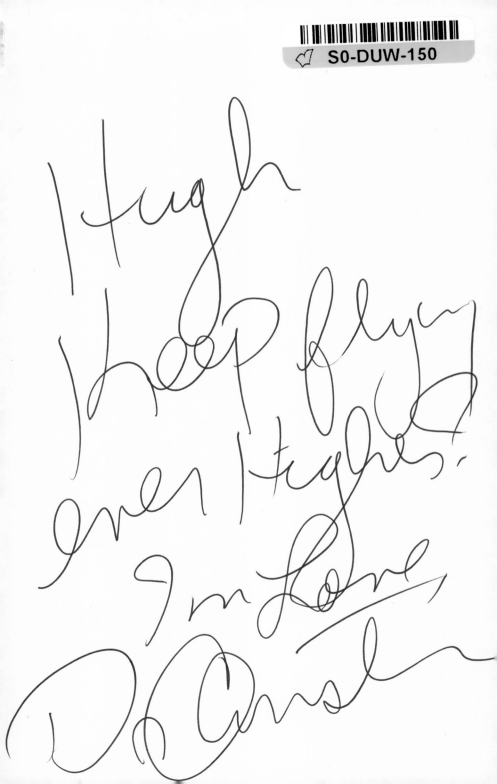

Hugh

keep flying

ever Hughes!

I'm Love

DeAnsl...

SOAR

Spiritual Guidance for
Overcoming Life's Turbulence

Rev. Christian Sørensen D.D.

~ Also by Rev. Christian Sørensen D.D.

CATCH THE SPIRIT *Riding the Waves of Life*

First Edition
Published November 2004

Library of Congress Cataloging-in-Publication Data

Sørensen, Christian C., 1960-
Catch the Spirit : flying through life : Rev. Christian C. Sørensen D.D.

Includes bibliographical references
ISBN 0-9726075-2-8
1. Spiritual life. 2. Flying—Miscellanea. 3. Self-actualization
(Psychology)—Religious aspects. I. Title.

Dedicated to
my wife Kalli,
who sends me soaring.

I would like to extend my deepest appreciation, thanks and love to:

Elizabeth Webster,
who spent countless hours transcribing
my words;

Tina Moreno,
for her patience in the editing process;

Beth Krippner,
for editing and proofreading;

Jeff Kahn,
at Kahn-Design.com for cover, book
layout & typographic design;

And all those people who have allowed
me to serve them through the years of
my ministry at Seaside Church.

Rev. Christian Sørensen D.D.

September 2004

C O N T E N T S

Introduction   XII-XIV

1. *Excess Baggage*   I
   What Are You Carrying?
   Excess Baggage of Resentments
   Excess Baggage of Outside Attachments
   Creating Excess Baggage
   Why Hold It?

2. *Risk Filing a New Flight Plan*   19
   Is It a Mistake?
   Prove It
   What's Stopping You?
   What's Stalling You?
   Into Bondage

3. *Enjoy Your Flight*   38
   Divine Winds
   Joy in the Vicinity of Work
   Inward Journey
   Stoned
   What Are You Seeking?
   Kick Off the Boots
   Great Thoughts
   Surprise of a Rainbow

4. *Weathering Storms and Turbulence*   57
   Can You Remember in the Storm?
   Getting Quiet
   Where Do You Dwell?
   Food for Flight
   Spirit's There
   A Loose Cannon
   Where Are You Lined Up?

5. *Fueled By Love*   82
   Intimate With the Inexhaustible
   How Do You Use the Fuel?
   Enough to Move Through the Ceiling
   How Much Can You Handle?

6. *In-flight Service*   96
   Adding Your Touch
   Flying With Heart
   Hearing the Control Tower
   What Are You Thinking?

7. *Trust the Flow*   III
   How Does Your Faith Go?
   Form Houses Consciousness
   Usurp God's Position Lately?
   What Do You Recognize?
   Expanding the Peripheral Vision
   Dueling With God?
   Not By Might
   Back Down or Back Up

8. *Jet Stream of Abundance*   135
   Zen of Abundance
   Increasing Up or Down?
   The Prodding Thorns
   I Shall Not Want

x

9. *Gaining Altitude–Christ Consciousness*   151
   What Are You Changing?
   Life's Daily Gifts
   The Heart Knows
   God and What?
   Where Are You Living?
   Espousing or Knowing
   Prayer of Faith
   From a Distance

10. *Coming in for a Landing*   171
   What Are You Looking At?
   What's Your Interpretation?
   More Than Meets the Eye
   Crack the Whip and Speak

11. *Flying Without a Plane—Immortality*   190
   What's Beyond?
   Good Package
   Part of the Whole
   Pushed or Pulled

Life Review Exercise   209

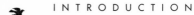
One fall morning I needed to get from San Diego, California, to Sedona, Arizona, for an early-morning meeting. The previous night had required my presence at a gathering, leaving few options outside the realm of bilocating. A good friend of mine, Dave Kilbourne, had been trying to get me up in his experimental airplane. I knew this was the ideal time to take him up on his offer. Little did I realize his "long E-Z" was smaller than my dining room table with its nose on the ground and propeller in the rear (a propeller, by the way, which needed to be hand-started).

When I squeezed into the back seat of the cockpit, I read a placard stating, "Passenger beware, this aircraft does not meet standard aviation requirements." I was a bit apprehensive as this fiberglass cylinder lifted off to the East. I remember looking down at the sunrise, the glorious morning colors of the desert, and experiencing the free feeling of being aloft. I watched individual houses and communities with roads connecting them merge into an orderly pattern as the winds off the Pacific carried us to our destination. Ernest Holmes, the founder of Religious Science, wrote in his book, *The Science of Mind,* "The world of multiplicity does not contradict the world of Unity, for the many live in the one." From my new airborne vantage point, it became apparent that an elevated perspective helps one to see our natural connectedness. It's a powerful metaphor to live by.

When we touched down on the spectacular Red Rock Mesa in Sedona an hour-and-a-half later (using less than ten gallons of gas, which makes for inexpensive transportation), I knew I was hooked on learning how to fly myself through life. On the return flight, I was sold on the concept of becoming a pilot. Little did I realize the rich lessons in store for me. I had to deal with my worthiness as people questioned, "How could a minister afford such a luxury?" I also had to deal with others' fears as they anxiously asked, "Haven't you heard about the latest plane crash?" Finally, when it came to exam time, I had to deal with my own concerns about passing, since I hadn't taken a test in two decades.

As I psyched myself up for the written exam, I remembered one of the driving reasons to get a pilot's license was to visit my wife's dad, Verle, who lived in Kanab, Utah. A ten-hour drive was about to become an easy two-hour flight and the sense of separation would dissolve. Kalli loved her papa dearly and seeing him was always a top priority. When Verle heard of my plans to pilot, he couldn't have been more thrilled and proud. He said he had no doubt in my ability and could hardly wait for me to take him up for a flight. I passed the written exam with flying colors.

The week before my actual checkout flight (with the examiner next to me in the cockpit), Kalli's sister, her daughter and four cats relocated to San Diego and were staying with us. As Spirit would have it, we all walked in together one evening from a beach bonfire to find a message on our answering machine from the Kanab coroner. He stated that Verle had died and he was in possession of the body, and asked what Kalli and her sister wanted to do with it. The agonized cries of Verle's daughters as they collapsed in my arms will live in me forever. The next day, Kalli and her sisters solemnly piled into the car for an unexpected trip to Utah. After church service the next day, Dave flew me out to be with them. With grace and dignity, Verle's three daughters lovingly went through what most of us have had, or will have, to deal with at one time or another.

The following day, upon our return from Utah, I was scheduled for my checkout flight. I remember feeling that perhaps this wasn't the appropriate time for what was supposed to be a special event. Kalli, who had lovingly supported me through my many whimsical doings, pulled her papa's denim coat out of a bag on this chilly morning and said, "Wear this. You know he supported your dream!" I felt Verle's support from the heavens as I successfully flew to receive my license that day.

Kalli's words on that morning continue to cloak me as I fly through life. I know the Spirit continues to support my dreams, just as the heavenly Father continues to support your dreams. Exactly what lies in your course of flight, no one knows. But I do know that whatever you encounter on the journey, you'll receive all the help you'll ever need from the in-flight instructions. You need only learn from the wonderful analogies life has tailor-made for you!

Enjoy your flight.

Rev. Christian Sørensen D.D.
Encinitas, California

SOAR

*Spiritual Guidance for Overcoming
Life's Turbulence*

CHAPTER ONE

I

EXCESS BAGGAGE

When checking in at the airport, you're asked,
"Are you carrying anything anyone has given you?"
What a great question to ask yourself in life!
Are you carrying anything anyone has given you?

The steady hum of airport noise was pierced by the sudden clamor of objects clattering to the floor, followed instantly by a woman's wail of distress. Next came the loud thud of her carry-on luggage hitting the tile, then her groan. Looking up, I saw a petite woman crouched down trying to gather her things. I'd seen her earlier; it would've been hard not to notice the well-dressed woman with a look of fierce concentration as she walked into the airport right in front of me, pushing a cart full of luggage that obviously weighed as much as she did. Getting up from the chair in front of the gate for my flight, I went over to try to help her, nearly falling over several curlers that rolled straight at me from her now-scattered belongings. Picking them up, I saw that the woman's carry-on bag—one of three once in arms, but now on the floor—appeared to have literally burst! Frantically she tried to gather her things and find a way to squeeze them back inside the bag—the pile of stuff was twice as big as the bag itself. In the midst of her harried repacking, the frazzled woman looked startled when I bent down to pick up a tube of lipstick, handed it to her and offered, "Would you like some help?" She wiped wisps of what was once her perfectly styled hair back from her face and gave me a look of dismay. "Oh, yes," she answered, her tone utterly beseeching. Gratefully grabbing the curlers, she put them in one of those electric curling kits women use, closed the plastic case and crammed it in the bag. She continued to cram her bag with handfuls of stuff: a curling iron (yes, a curling iron, when she already had curlers—go figure), a blow-dryer (apparently her hair was a priority), no fewer than four bulging makeup bags, three bathing suits, a large beach towel, a knitted cap, scarf and gloves, a small travel iron, and an array of vitamins, over-the-counter medicines, lotions and creams. "Oh, all this junk," she lamented. "But you never know what you might need. It might be hot; it might be cold. You should see all the bags I already checked in." Picking up some antacids, she rambled, "Never know when you might get an upset stomach—or a headache," she added, picking up some pain reliever. Everything finally back in the bulging bag, she stood up, hoisting it over her shoulder. Its matching counterpart, a bulging purse, was draped over her other shoulder. "Thank you," she said, looking frantically down the hall, then glancing at her watch. "Oh, no! I hope I haven't missed my flight!"

"Well, have a great vacation," I said. Startled, she looked back at me and corrected, "Oh, I'm not going on vacation. I'm on my way to a convention for the weekend."

A weekend! I'd seen all she'd brought into the airport; she looked like she was packed up for a long vacation—or moving. A few minutes later, I heard a distinctive clatter and a now-familiar wail of distress from down the corridor in the direction she'd been headed.

Even aviation regulations, for very good reason, guard against an aircraft's carrying excess baggage. Not only does it weigh down the aircraft, it throws the plane off balance, making a safe, smooth flight unlikely at best. As an added precaution, placards are posted in planes to indicate weights and balances.

Now you'd think people would pay attention to those inner regulations that warn them against carrying excess baggage—such as fear, resentment, hatred, prejudice, insecurity or doubt—through their lives. Unfortunately people often don't comply with those inner placards and safety regulations. They refuse to listen to the alarms of the sense that go off within, attempting to guide them in their lives.

Metaphysics works with that feeling—the inner sense. It's not about the words. It's about soaring to a higher altitude—soaring beyond your circumstance or story, leaving the limiting luggage you carry (about yourself and others) far behind. Yet there are some who store their excess baggage in consciousness. Consequently they're thrown off balance, unable to soar smoothly through life's ideal altitudes. They persist in hanging on to burdensome baggage. Some people drag it around for a lifetime, talking about it, mulling it over in their minds, scrupulously making certain it's right there in the cargo hold of their consciousness.

What Are You Carrying?

When checking in at the airport, you're asked, "Are you carrying anything anyone has given you?" What a great question to ask yourself in life! Are you carrying anything anyone has given you? Are you carrying any put-downs, inadequacies or phobias others have instilled in you?

While gardening this week, I noticed some squash seeds I'd planted were popping up, starting to show themselves. But there was this one spot where nothing was happening—no sprout, no growth. I looked to the seedling brothers and sisters that were doing okay, then back to the empty patch in my garden. Furrowing gently around the spot, I found a big dirt clod right under the surface of the soil. I knocked away the dirt clod, broke it up, and there underneath it sprouted this twisted and contorted seedling.

When I think about the effects of lugging excess baggage through life, it seems obvious the clod represents our fears, prejudices and adversities. Those things weigh us down, allowing us to twist and contort our minds and our thinking, and to move away from Faith, instead of knowing with a greater sense of assurance as we move toward our greater destiny.

God hasn't given us the spirit of fear, as Timothy wrote in the Bible, but one of love. If you are experiencing fear—if you are experiencing that kind of energy—it's time to realize maybe you are off course. Maybe you should take a look at the baggage you're dragging around on your flight, and see what has been holding you down and throwing you off balance.

Excess Baggage of Resentments

I like the well-known Hawaiian saying, "If you want to enjoy the rainbows, you have to put up with the rain." Well, if you want to enjoy the rainbows and the beauty in life, you have to reach a point where you take stock of what you've packed away in your cargo hold. So many times, when this cargo includes negative situations, you claim them in a way that is counterproductive by saying, "This is who I am." You should get off it and say instead, "Hey, I am not this experience; I am a child of God. I am a center through which the Divine expresses. So there was some rain; it brought forth a rainbow. I'm not going to get all worked up and filled with anger and resentment and bitterness over this, because doing that pulls me straight down out of the flow, and there goes my creativity, peace, love and well-being!"

Back in school, one of my best buddies wronged me. Upset and angry, I wanted revenge. I was going to get him back, to do worse than what was done to me.

Out in the schoolyard, I noticed a furry piece of cactus with soft burrs that itch like fiberglass if they get into the skin when broken off the plant. Looking at it, I came up with a plan: I decided I was going to drop it down my friend's shirt and squish it into his back. (Boys will be boys.) So I put the porcupine piece in my pocket and carried it around all day, waiting for the right moment to get even. Every time I moved, the spines pricked me. Finally, at the end of the day, when I took the cactus out of my pocket, all the needles were gone. When I pulled down my pant leg, however, there they all were—embedded in my thigh. I had held on to the revenge and anger throughout the whole day and I was the one who got stuck as a result.

When you take a look at the excess baggage in your cargo hold, what you'll come to discover is the weight of such resentments and insecurities. As with me and my cactus, resentments or insecurities can even seem justified. But in the end, you are the one who is injured when you hang on to them. Insecurities come from a place of insufficiency, which is the result of a separation from the infinite Source that seeks to express Itself through you.

We tend to visualize our fears, the realm of phenomena and outside effects, instead of knowing the truth and slowly listening to our higher self speaking. In this knowing and listening, we will hear not only inner flight regulations but also flight directions for the smoothest, grandest, most exciting flight imaginable.

Aristotle said (I'm paraphrasing), "To become angry is an easy thing to do, but to become angry at the right person, at the right time, for the right purpose, at the right degree, in the right way—that's not an easy thing to do." Within life, situations arise. Sometimes you have to put up with rain so you can have the beauty and the growth, so you can deepen your understanding and begin to expand, freeing yourself of the excess baggage and moving beyond what's going on in your present life. But sometimes people hold on to the persecution of another person in their mind—the resentment, the anger and the bitterness. Those kinds of things will separate them from the very Source. How can you be one with God if you're thinking ungodly thoughts? Think about that for a moment. How can you be into loving your neighbor and hatred at the same time—or be into the Christ consciousness and bitterness at the same time? It doesn't work, does it? Of course it doesn't work! You've got to be able to let go of your excess baggage, throw away bitterness, and move beyond your story. Then the skies will open up. You will become the channel through which God presents Divine ideas you may not have known even existed.

If the warning lights are going off and you're sensing your higher self warning that you are holding on to excess baggage from some prior time in history—if you are so ticked off at yourself or another person that you've got energy going for that activity—as the Course in Miracles says, "Forgiveness is the only sane response." Forgiveness allows you to soar and gain altitude, granting an elevated perspective on the situation. Forgiveness is not a wimpy act. It's a very powerful, decisive action, eliminating judgment and entrapment. It opens the cargo door and dumps the excess baggage, allowing you to ascend to the proper course. Eliminating the shackles, which keep a person bound to past experiences, creates a wonderful space and movement in which miracles and spiritual connections with our Divine Source occur. Offering the ability to be one who has witnessed the presence of

God in all places, it allows peace instead of anger. Now where do you want to be flying? Forgiveness is the only sane response.

Excess Baggage of Outside Attachments

People can become pretty attached to their baggage, especially some fancy embroidered kind. In fact, they may even come to believe it's their treasure, or a vital part of who they are. One thing that creates resistance to letting go of such excess is getting caught up in trying to hold on to what you've finally created. Such thinking asserts, "I worked all my life to create this house, this car, this job, this relationship."

I want you to know the things we are experiencing here in this life are only on loan. God's only rented them to you for a short time. Eventually you're going to have to let go and surrender them all. If you are in need of them at this point in your life you don't have to give them up. It would be ridiculous for me to give up my pants as I stood before a seminar crowd—I need them. If there are "things" supporting you in your life right now, it may not be appropriate to give them up. I'm not saying "give" means give up everything. Of course not! There may be some things serving you well at this moment. I'm not talking about giving up those things. What I'm talking about is being in the flow and giving up the attachment—the need to hold on to things—because as long as you are into attachment to possessions (which at death you're going to have to give up anyway), you are putting your energy on the outside of yourself. As long as your energy is going on the outside to things, you're missing out on the fact that it is the *inside* that creates! If you have strong feelings about the way things are supposed to look outside, you're missing out on the inner connection, which creates them in the first place. On the inside, the Infinite expresses Itself. On the inside, we connect with the Source. If you truly believe God is Infinite, and Spirit is within you, then what you have is infinite—infinite potential. Coming from your Inner Source, from a place of flow, you're going to watch a wealth unfold in your life; you'll have no desire to carry all the extra baggage, because you'll find all your needs met at your destination.

There was a story in the *San Diego Union Tribune* about Amy Higgs, an elderly widow who was about 70 years of age. She always carried around a brown paper bag with strings tied around it. Inside this bag was 85,000 dollars in stacks of either hundreds or fifties. She didn't trust banks, so she carried her sack of money with her wherever she went. The story showed up in the newspaper because one evening, when she was in a local drugstore, she left it on the counter. When she realized her loss and called the drugstore, they had already closed but said they would reopen for her. Unable to locate her missing bag, she reported the loss of her money to the police. The newspaper went on to say she often had left the bag in other places and it had always come back to her. This time, however, it was gone for good. To me, it's a classic case of the fear people have. They don't trust, so they hoard what they've got instead of using what they have. When they hold on to it, all of a sudden it becomes a burden—excess baggage—and they become grounded by their fear of losing it.

Creating Excess Baggage

Sometimes what people carry around is their own preconceived stuff; it's what they've become comfortable with. There was a guy from the Sierras who moved to Kansas. He built a big, beautiful house for himself, with a huge picture window overlooking hundreds of miles of open range. As he looked out the window, he complained, "There's nothing out there to look at."

About the same time, there was a man from Kansas who moved to the Sierras. He built a big, beautiful house for himself, with a huge picture window overlooking the grand Sierras. He grumbled, "I can't see anything because the mountains are in the way."

What are you looking through? What are you looking at? How are you looking? Are you willing to let go and just be—to open up your heart and your soul and experience the gifts of Spirit? When flying, it is essential to continually scan the skies and see everything you can. It's not about complaining about what you see, but observing it all.

I've come to understand that part of what keeps many people from doing this is their having been hurt in the past. They've become vulnerable and squashed; they have loved and been wounded. It tends to make the hinges on the door of the cargo hold so rusty that they are afraid to open them, afraid to take a look inside and toss out their excess baggage. But only in so doing are you able to cruise to new heights through the open skies of eternity.

Over a period of time, fuel left sitting in a gas tank becomes contaminated and ineffective, and can fail you in a critical moment. Our spirit and our soul want to soar with ecstasy, intimacy and love. But when not used—not given or received—the fear of loving is the contaminant that denies the bliss. Did you ever get up out of a chair after sitting there all day or all week? Did you notice how slowly you moved? As you begin to make those movements of greater love for yourself and others, you may also move slowly at first. But in going forward you'll find you're gaining speed and altitude, all the while becoming magically refueled by the untainted fuel of the very love you burn.

Some of the painful experiences that pull us off course aren't happening in our lives today; they happened to us as children, or in previous relationships, or with old bosses, and we've kept them alive by feeding them in the barren cargo holds of our minds.

Watch little children; listen to their laughter and their fun. Think of how important it is for their parents to create the safest environment possible. They step out into the world and sometimes their experiences out there make a definite impact.

I want to share with you a poem about a little boy:

He's Just a Little Boy

He stands at the plate with his heart pounding fast.
The bases are loaded and the die has been cast.
Mom and Dad cannot help him, he stands all alone.
A hit, at this moment, would send the team home.
The ball meets the plate, he swings and he misses.
There's a groan from the crowd with some "boos" and some "hisses."
A thoughtless voice cries, "Strike out the bum!"
Tears fill his eyes; the game's no longer fun.
So open your hearts and give him a break,
For it's moments like this, a man you can make.
Please keep this in mind when you hear someone forget.
He's just a little boy and not a man quite yet.

That little boy is still inside. You may be an adult in this earthly drag, but the child who had those experiences is still just as alive and aware as he was then. You may not be in a small body any more. Who you are is in a bigger package, but you had these soul experiences. Give yourself a break; love yourself, encourage yourself and tell yourself what a good job you have done this far in your life. We've all made some blunders and mistakes and are going to make some more. We've also stepped into those magical moments when we connected, when we were open, when the Spirit flowed and the ecstasy of the Divine showed up in body. This happened because we were willing to let go of all the excess baggage and become intimate in the present moment with the true source of energy—the infinite fullness.

Author Alan Watts wrote, "We do not come into this world. We come out of it—as leaves from a tree; as the ocean waves; the universe peoples. Every individual is an expression of the whole realm of nature; a unique action of the total universe."

We come out of that. The whole universe is our home, the place where we grow and evolve. The uterus isn't the only womb. The heart helps to raise the child that is still alive within you. If you find yourself at a tough spot in life, such as a relationship that is of a challenging nature, be willing to know that in that very moment resides the home of the Divine. You can remember. The memory can be activated. Something wonderful is seeking to express through you, but you've got to exercise your choice to get back on bearing.

Why Hold It?

When you inventory your excess baggage, you'll find what you've stored in the cargo hold is the past. My theory on that: Let the past be done! Close the chapter! There is nothing you can do about the past. There's a lot you can do about the present. There's a lot you can do about the future, because the future is created from the present, but most are creating it from the past. But the past is done; there is nothing you can do about it. Learn from it and move on. Why carry it around with you?

If you want to hold on to those prenatal influences you may

have had before you got going and complain about how your childhood got messed up, giving these things storage space that can better be used for precious, empowering cargo, that's your prerogative. You can do that. Instead of focusing on the joy and the abundance and the Divine realization, you can allow those past negatives to fill your consciousness and awareness, and life will say, "Absolutely!" What you choose to focus on, you get to experience. That's the way it works. We experience the unfolding of consciousness. What if, rather than choosing to focus on the heavy stuff, you choose to focus on the Presence, the love and the joy? You would then experience new altitudes where there is well-being. Many people take an hour or an hour-and-a-half once a week on Sunday morning just to experience the Presence. It's beautiful! Imagine how wonderful it would be if you took an hour every day to allow Spirit in your consciousness, ten minutes five times a day, or five minutes ten times a day. Then you'd be excited to open your packages to share the gifts you've been carrying.

Standing in line at a small airport cafeteria, I noticed a person in front of me and just sensed he was in pain. Literally, it was something you could feel. His T-shirt hovered just above his navel and his potbelly hung out over his dirty sweats. Now, there is nothing wrong with being overweight if you're content with the ramifications upon your body, but you could tell this person was not happy with life. His hair was matted and unwashed. He didn't have an appropriate aroma or fragrance. He was buying a huge bag of greasy potato chips, one of those prewrapped, processed, chocolate chip cookies and he had a rolled-up tabloid magazine clenched in one of his hands. Any one of these on its own might be okay but, as I mentioned, I could feel his pain. My sense was that this individual didn't care. There was hopelessness, as if he didn't feel he had control of his life any more and was stuck in whatever pattern was going on in his life—as if he felt powerless and was attempting to lose himself in the junk food and junk reading material.

I wanted to pray for this guy, but I wouldn't invade another person's world and say, "Hey, I'm going to pray for you without permission." But it's okay to see the presence of God there, so I said, "Hey, God, come on out. Come on out of the apparent hopelessness here." I had to take my thinking out of the junk food thoughts and choose the whole food, which enriches the environment in which I live.

I know many of us at times have tried to lose our feelings in food, or lose our minds in reading, TV, drugs, sex, computers, gambling or something else. In order to avoid getting intimate with our true selves, we choose to fill our minds with different kinds of garbage. For whatever reason, sometimes there is a sense in people's lives that they're not in control—that they don't have choice any more: "I'm stuck with this lot in life."

It doesn't matter where you are in your life, or what is going on in your world or in your body. It doesn't matter what your upbringing, background, education, or whether or not you came from a dysfunctional home, you still have a choice to dump the baggage.

I urge you not to give away that God-given power of choice. Choose to become intimate with yourself and come to recognize that no matter where you are, what condition is going on, or what experience you've had, you are still heir apparent to the Kingdom. The Kingdom of God is at hand. This Kingdom has been given to you—yes, to you! You are entitled to the fullness, but you must find something that allows you to recognize that your estimated time of arrival is now, for in this moment is the home of God. Discover you have the courage and conviction to cross the threshold to eternity where the fullness of Spirit is seeking to express Itself as you. You must be willing to be vulnerable enough to open your eyes and believe your journey has led you home. This is when you'll come to experience love.

In his book, *The Science of Mind*, Ernest Holmes wrote:

> *We should learn to let go of our mistakes and remember them no longer against ourselves. Nothing is gained by holding to past errors. The best thing to do is to let go of and forget them altogether. It is scientific to consciously let go all our troubles. It is most unwise to hold them. Some will say that it's right that we should suffer for our past errors. It is right that we should suffer; but we have already done so and will continue to do so until we pay the last farthing. But the last farthing is paid when we let go and trust in the Law of Good. It's impossible for a sane person to believe that God delights in condemning or damning anyone. God is natural goodness and eternal loving kindness, and holds nothing against anyone.*

We should suffer until we've paid the last farthing? That's a quarter of a penny over in England. The last farthing has been paid as soon as you're willing to give up the baggage. It is up to you to close that chapter of the book in your life. Just like any good book that makes more sense as you get into it, life makes more sense as you move more into it. As you are willing to close the chapter and be done with it, allowing your heart, your soul, your mind, your consciousness and your whole being to be free, there is greater space for the Spirit to bring forth Its gifts. There's more space for you to begin to experience those nuances you are coming to understand, so you can see the presence of God in all the places within your life. The presence of God is shouting to you, but you have to be willing to let go of not only the bad, but also the good. Let go of it all, in this, the human life. As you do, the "is-ness" of Spirit remains—the good, the wholeness, the abundance, the ease and the loving kindness. You have to be willing to open the cargo door and allow the vacuum force to naturally suck out the garbage.

There's a story about the ice flow in Niagara Falls. In the springtime, when the ice is flowing down the river, chunks of ice are loaded with seagulls. The birds just have a ball floating down the river on their free cruise, dining on a scrumptious buffet of frozen fish carcasses. Then at the last moment, they spread their wings and fly off before the flowing ice goes over the falls. Somebody was recounting a story to me about one bird that was enjoying his meal. All the other birds took off, but he stayed on till the very last moment before the ice was going to go over. He lifted his wings to fly and you could see he was using all his energy flapping his wings, and it was as if the ice came out of the water with him. But he had held on too long; his feet had frozen to the iceberg. As it went over, it took the bird crashing down to the bottom of the falls. What are you holding on to in your life that it's time to let go? What excess baggage is weighing you down? Where in your life is it time to unload and let go?

Many times, what ends up being excess baggage is the guilt we hang on to for what we view as our past mistakes. Guilt is self-inflicted nonsense that allows us to keep on doing what we know is not right. It was Shakespeare who admonished us in his *Winter's Tale,* "Do as heaven has done, forget your evils." Instead of using the word "evils," I just can't help being filled with the thought of "mistakes." Let us forget our mistakes. Let's let them go. As I look upon my life, I realize there are some things I've done that I wouldn't do again. But I've realized, for some reason, at that time

I felt it was the right thing to do. Whatever those mistakes may have been, whatever it is you may have done or wish you had not done, forget your mistakes and be willing to move on with your life. If you continue to carry those mistakes around, trying to make them who you are, they become part of the dangerous excess baggage hindering your flight.

In spite of all the warnings about excess baggage, fear, pain and insecurity being hindrances to one's flight, in spite of all the evidence of freedom and joy available through simply letting go, many times people would rather seek out others to unite behind them. It's not too hard to do; people often feel compelled to unite in adversity. They put energy into getting others to acknowledge their adversity, challenges, troubles and their "woe is me," and suck others into believing in the value of their baggage. You've heard of "the flavor of the month"? Well, this is like, "Who's the bad guy of the month?" Or what is the bad condition of the month? Who is it we do not like? What nation is it we are opposed to? What boss is not on our "good list"? Against whom in our relationship, or whom in our family, or whom in our nation, or whom on this planet do we want to unite in adversity, really generating fear and confusion, and begin to visualize exactly what we don't want to experience? Just tune into the tabloid frequency.

It's time to get off this kind of visualization and rise above the mob mentality! Let those who choose to wallow in the pain and burden of lugging their heavy baggage of fear and confusion do so, while you choose to place your faith in God and fly.

One way of getting rid of any excess baggage is to be absolutely in the present moment where God is. I have another way to help myself toss the baggage of a story I carry around about myself or someone else: If I find I'm telling the same story three times, I'm over my limit. At this point, a little baggage alarm goes off in my mind, saying, "Beep, beep, beep—Christian, time to unload this one." In our lives things happen and it's good to share and process experiences, but carrying those things around forever burdens us with unnecessary weight, and throws us off Life's divine flight course.

This big guy went out and bought himself a brand-new chainsaw. The salesman guaranteed him that this chainsaw would cut three cords of firewood a day. Excited with his purchase, the guy rushed home to cut some firewood. After a few days he came back to the salesman, exhausted, and said it was cutting only one cord of firewood a day. So the salesman took the chainsaw and pulled the cord. *Brrrrrrmmmm.* The guy stepped back, his mouth dropped open, his eyes lit up and he said, "What's that noise?"

Too many of us are trying to do this life alone, without guidance and support. We have the power inside us and yet we're out there trying to cut wood, do life, come up with a new plan of action all on our own without pulling the cord and allowing the energy of Spirit to move through us and others. You are not alone.

As we allow ourselves to become intimate with our spiritual self, through faith we will come to feel, recognize and experience freedom and balance of Spirit more and more in our lives. That's what it's all about: stepping into the spot where energy becomes so real and so pervasive it is our navigational force. As we become more intimately aware of our spirituality and less burdened by our earthly baggage, the energy stirring in our souls reveals itself in ever-greater and increasing ways, propelling us back on our course in currents of life.

I trust you'll personalize this in your life. I'm not just speaking abstractly here. Dump the excess baggage! Do not allow your mind to be dominated by the memories of mistakes, blunders, the times you stumbled, how you got hurt or dumped. Rather, go back to the place that is free of excess baggage, the place of knowing who you are is good enough. Have the faith of God, which is your expressing at your level of understanding—not a Faith in God, but a Faith *of* God. This brings power back into your life and allows you to plot your course, guiding you through challenges, new or old, allowing you to gain and maintain those higher altitudes!

CHAPTER TWO

RISK FILING A NEW FLIGHT PLAN

What have you done

in your life thus far?

Do you use these experiences

as reasons for your fear

of making a mistake?

Then I want you to consider:

there are no mistakes.

It's part of what took place;

see the larger picture, the elevated view.

Every pilot files a flight plan before lifting off the runway. It's easy to feel comfortable with a familiar flight plan, one you've flown over and over again. There may not be as much comfort—and may even be some fear—when filing a flight plan that's entirely new, involving a whole new destination or a more challenging flight course. The action of facing an unknown destination and landing requires a certain amount of risk.

When filing a new flight plan in the course of our journey through the skies of life, we often experience the same type of discomfort or fear in taking the risk of failure. We see the familiar as just that—familiar. We've learned how to cruise along on its course. Perhaps we don't soar, perhaps we don't reach those altitudes and destinations our hearts and souls long for, but we are able to cruise along on our familiar course. "Why risk the turbulence? Why risk the unknown? Why risk danger of failure?" we might reason. But in truth, the doubt manifesting in such reasoning is limiting—limiting the soul from soaring, limiting Spirit from expressing through you, and as you.

Thomas Edison said, "If we did all the things that we are capable of doing, we would literally astound ourselves." Doing those things means trusting Spirit and moving beyond fear of filing a new flight plan in our lives. Numerous times, I've flown over deserts where everything looked the same and I didn't know exactly where I was. Yet, surrendering to the fear, thus far I've always made it to my destination and taken in beautiful new views.

There were a couple of caterpillars crawling along the ground and they looked up at a butterfly flying through the air. One caterpillar said to the other, "You're never going to get me up in one of those contraptions."

Like the caterpillar, you may resist life, resist taking flight and becoming who you are meant to be. Yet those desires percolate inside you, urging you to lift off. What is necessary is to taxi up to the numbers for takeoff, rev the engine, give it full throttle, release the brakes and lift off. No matter what level you're at with your spiritual growth and your spiritual evolution, there is more. It is higher, richer and fuller. Our desire begins to put us in places that allow us to see and understand the nuances of our lives. Letting go of resistance means courageously taking our feet off the brakes in order to reach greater destinations.

Being interviewed while sweeping through the playoffs one year, taking the Chicago Bulls to best record in basketball, Michael Jordan said, "I never think about the consequences of missing a big shot." It's just not part of his thinking. If he misses the big shot he gets to deal with it, but thinking about it is not the way his mind works. When it comes right down to the crunch, the important moment, his thinking is not based upon fear. Instead, he thinks, "Give me the ball. I'm the one who want to come through." He doesn't think about making a mistake or missing a shot; he steps out in belief, knowing he'll come through.

Is It a Mistake?

Are you allowing your fear of making a mistake to keep you from filing a new flight plan? Is it something you just don't want to risk? Let's take a look at the word, the thought and the emotion behind a "mistake" and view it from a new perspective.

Henry Ford had some great antics at the beginning of his career. Some might say he made mistakes—we're talking semantics here. As you may have heard, he forgot to put a reverse gear in the first car he built. He built the car in a garage with a regular door, and the door wasn't big enough for him to get the car out. If you go back to his place, you can see the building where they actually cut a hole out of the wall so they could get this car to go forward out of the building where it was built. Was this a mistake? Well, it was certainly an event.

Vincent Van Gogh painted hundreds of works in his day, but sold only one painting in his whole life. Nearly a century after he took his life, collectors are paying unprecedented sums for his work. What a shame Van Gogh never got to see a cent of it. But wouldn't it have been even more of a shame if he hadn't painted, if he'd quit, deciding he was making a mistake and wasn't doing it right? Certainly it would have been a greater shame if he'd quit because he felt he was making a mistake—deciding his new style and concept, the new flight plan he was filing with the new kind of art he was creating wasn't right—and had stopped right there.

The first plane the Wright brothers built was hardly classified as a success. Yet in creating that bucket of bolts and trying to get it off the ground, they weren't making a mistake. Alexander Graham Bell's first telephones definitely wouldn't hold up to Bell's present lab standards. But what he foisted off on us as a telephone back in those early days led to the massive global linkage we have going on in our world right now. It wasn't a mistake. The Wright brothers and Alexander Graham Bell assisted us in getting to where we are today.

We are living in an accelerated time, where we are getting many life lessons. It used to take people a whole lifetime to learn a particular soul lesson. Now we are being given many lifetimes of experience in just one life. It may be you've learned what you were meant to learn from a particular partner or job and it's time to move on. When arriving at a destination it's sometimes appropriate to have a new team on board for the next journey. If you've been filing the same route and you are bored, it may also be an indication that that leg of your journey is complete.

What have you done in your life thus far? Do you use these experiences as reasons for your fear of making a mistake? Then I want you to consider: There are no mistakes. It's part of what took place; see the larger picture, the elevated view. It was an event—like Ford's creation. It was just an event. But if the energy you put into it begins to shape it and make it dark or negative or judgmental, you've put the brakes on the Divine flow, stopping the creative energy. The creative energy of God is what brings the new ideas, what allows you to develop a space shuttle from what was once an airplane, and was a Model T before being an airplane. But if you sit there in judgment and say, "Oh man, this is bad. How could I have done that? What was I thinking?" all of a sudden the head, the mind, the energy gets pulled off into an entirely different direction.

So I recommend you just say, "Hey, thank you, God." Offer up your work, whatever it is that comes out of you and say, "I'm grateful. It's just a bucket of bolts, but so what? Forgot to put the hole in! What was I thinking? But thank you, God." Start looking at the people in your world and start saying, "Thank you for the wonderful people, these generous folks, these wonderful friends, and these friendships, for the opportunities, for the richness of God to shine forth from these people in my world. Thank you, God, for the beauty I see all around me. Thank you, God, for the possibilities of the glory, the wonder and the greatness that can come forward in my life!" You'll discover an exciting outcome—it works! You then become a witness; you become a beholder of the Presence of God making Itself known on your new and exciting course. You become a spectator to the Divine play, to the Divine interaction; you become an experience through which the activity of God is moving. You can't help but be lifted out of some degree of humanoid that you've been existing in—the one sitting in judgment of those mistakes or of those experiences. You cannot help but be forcefully lifted to a higher elevation of spiritual understanding—an awareness of what has transpired thus far in your life. We've all done things that in retrospect we wish we hadn't done, but we did the best we could at the time. So what? It got you to where you are today. You're in a good place, you're reading this book and you're coming to experience the Presence of God even more in your life. You're being lifted, and as you're lifted, you're relieved of the pressure of attempting to make it happen with the means of your mind. You're relieved of the consumption of trying to demonstrate healing, trying to demonstrate something with your own power, and your own ability and your own affirmations.

It's a feeling, a connection that's not in your head. You know when you're in your own head, looking for solutions in your mind, it's like trying to talk to a Walkman you brought along on your flight and hoping for a reply, instead of connection with the control tower. And you're expecting the Walkman to answer you with directions? Give me a break! While the mind just chatters away, there is a Soul, a Spirit inside you that knows there are no mistakes, no matter what experience you find yourself in. You got that? No matter what—not "all experiences except this one that I'm in right now," but all experiences!

Abraham Lincoln failed his way to success, and he said, "The man who is incapable of making a mistake is incapable of anything." Are you stuck in that place of fear? Are you afraid to risk building a car in a garage because you're sure it's going to be trapped inside the garage? Afraid to say words you know your heart is yearning to say? Afraid to express yourself in a relationship in the way your heart wants you to express? Afraid to say those things that need to be said in a business setting, or to move boldly to put together a contract or deal? Have you become incapacitated by the fear of the supposed mistake? If so, allow yourself to realize this truth: You cannot make a mistake. Even if things don't turn out exactly as you envisioned, taking action is the first step. It breaks the inertia and gets things going. You've got to move into that activity by releasing the brakes and giving it full throttle. File the new flight plan and take off for a new, exciting location!

Prove It

Performers are in a risky position. They don't know if their voice is going to be working, if they are going to hit the note, or if the other performers are going to be backing them or hitting their marks. An artist putting some strokes on a canvas doesn't know how it's going to be received—talk about vulnerability—yet he says, "This is me expressing."

Have you ever seen a person walking down the street wearing a wonderful necklace made out of bold pieces of stones or tinted glass? Obviously they picked it up at a street fair. Looking at it, you thought, "Who would ever wear that?" and you stick with your fine chain or pearls because you just don't have the guts to wear something brighter. It's stunning to see it confidently worn by a person who has the guts and is willing to take the risk.

Every Sunday I stand up in front of my congregation without knowing if Spirit's going to fill my mouth with the words and the room with energy that day, but I trust. It takes risking within your life. It takes willingness to step out trusting Spirit. It's the action, not just saying, "God is love," and speaking fine, flowery principles. Of course God's going to provide. Life helps those who help themselves. God will show up when we take the action, when we are willing to step outside of where we have been, based upon both principle and stepping into the flow of action.

In New Thought we know principles of truth such as, "God is wonderful and abundant and flowing, yet I still have to open up to it." We have to do something with it. So often we become passive with these great principles, which doesn't necessarily make them work in our lives.

A street performer shared an interesting story from his childhood. When he was young, his dad was a minister who always said, "God will provide." But there wasn't much income in the house and they went through a great deal of poverty. So one day at the age of ten, when his family was struggling for some food, this street performer grabbed a hat and ran out into the city. He set the hat open on the ground and began to perform. When the hat became half-filled with money, he decided he'd done well enough and went home. Before going into the house, he took all the coins and stuffed them in his dark, curly hair, in the cuffs of his pants and up his sleeves.

Walking into the house, he said, "Mom, shake me."

"What are you taking about?" his mother replied, and the only thing she shook was her head as she chided, "I'm too busy." (Does this sound familiar? When God is calling do you sometimes give the same reply?)

"Oh, Mom, shake me!" he insisted, persisting until his mom shook him and all the coins fell out of his hair, hat and clothes.

"You know, Dad is right; God will provide," he told her. "It's also true God helps those who help themselves."

You must plot your course and take the action in your life to implement it if Spirit is going to show up. It is great to read this material, but in order to use it you have to apply it—to be willing to believe when things don't look like they should be believed in. It's great taking classes, but I'll tell you, we do not become spiritual by receiving a diploma or a license. One does not become ordained through an institute; one becomes ordained by the presence of God. One becomes more spiritually in touch when one begins to have the experience. You use spiritual principles by getting in touch, thinking, feeling and practicing them. Classes are wonderful and diplomas are terrific, just as long as they are rites of something going on at a deeper level. They're great when they represent a passage to a greater understanding, so one has the experience in his life. It's about moving out of the head and into the heart. Then God indoctrinates one.

As I share my revelations, experiences or insights, I share my experiences that might help illustrate or help one's thinking move to a higher place, but one begins to know the truth as they live it. God helps those who help themselves. It is about the experience. It doesn't do us any good to have a flight plan and never take off, to go around shouting, "Hey, Spirit is going to take me to greater destinations in life," and then sit home and just wait. It is essential that we begin to prove this in our lives, to actually become airborne.

T.S. Eliot wrote, "Only those who risk going too far could ever possibly find out how far they can go." Only those who are willing to go too far are ever going to find out where their limit is. Have you ever pushed yourself to find the stuff you have inside you? Unless a skier falls a couple of times in the course of the day, he's not pushing himself to the edge, to his limit. Well, in our lives if we're not falling sometimes, we haven't gotten to the edge of our capabilities—our possibilities are infinite. It's okay to fall, to make a mistake. You pick yourself back up. You get on the skis. You get back on track. You start going. You find your bearings.

What's Stopping You?

Here's a game for you to practice. I like this game. Try to figure out what is the best you could experience here. You just go for the best in your world and have fun with it. If you're going for a job, and there's one position available and 500 applicants, you go for it. Put your name in there; have fun with it. So what if you don't get it? If you're throwing a party and there is someone you really want to have come to your party—a big star or someone—invite them. Right now we are not receiving all the good in our lives just because we haven't asked for it. It's true! What are you not asking for from Life so It can source you, so It can take care of you?

There are entire anthologies of people who started in horrible situations and have become multimillionaires. I read stories of those who are born with deformed bodies and just cannot function physically and yet who have achieved great successes in their lives. I listen to those who have come from broken, dysfunctional families and who are now in almost ideal situations. I read and hear compelling stories that deeply touch my heart. I sit there amazed at these stories of individuals who have called upon the presence of God, but the more amazing part to me is not that God has answered the call—it's how all of us are not calling upon the Spirit at the same level in our lives. Isn't it more amazing that some have chosen to wimp out?

I read about a guy whose face is absolutely deformed, yet he fell in love with his soul mate and they're happily married. He chose a greater flight plan than much of society would have thought possible. Other people are complaining they don't look good enough, their bodies aren't hard enough, they're not thin enough or they're not buffed enough. I heard of someone who had no legs and came from a place of poverty to become a multimillionaire. Meanwhile, others are walking on two legs into yet another prosperity seminar, listening to principles that, if applied after the first seminar they had gone to, would already have them living their dreams.

Toward the end of her career, Dr. Peggy Bassett, a great Minister of Religious Science, President Emeritus of that movement at the time, ended up in a wheelchair. A lady of great dignity, unable to speak clearly, but willing to put herself before the people in a wheelchair, she shared from her heart and moved people in a deep way. Yet, I listen to individuals afraid to join Toastmasters because of their fear of stumbling or bumbling with their words. Using this power requires plotting your course and taking off beyond your fear.

People tend to be afraid to move in their lives because they are not going to look good or they think they are going to fail. So what? So what if you fail? No big deal! You pick yourself up again, and you begin to apply yourself. This is how you use It in your life. You become willing to go for it and attempt to be all you were intended to be because the Kingdom of Heaven is at hand. It's not going to come someday. It is here for us to live now. You know, this Kingdom of Heaven is not a place we are going to reach in some ethereal aspect of our being. We are not going to meet God any more after we leave here than we are able to today. It's omnipresent. *Thy kingdom's come.* It's here now. It is about living in a Spiritual way, here on Earth.

How do you use It? You begin to call upon the Power. You don't need to be impoverished. You don't need to be in a body that doesn't work. Call upon it! Once again, the amazing part is people forget to call upon Spirit. Take the risk—create a new plan, file it and fly!

What's Stalling You?

Joanne, a young single mother, noticed a lump in her breast. She was busy taking care of her ten-year-old daughter, and was certain it was just some sort of hormone-induced cyst. Initially Joanne put off going to the doctor, but eventually became concerned enough to have it checked out. The doctor ordered a mammogram. The results weren't encouraging, and the doctor ordered a biopsy, which indicated Joanne definitely had breast cancer. He told her the best thing that could be done for her at this point was to undergo chemotherapy, so this young, vibrant single mother went through the process of those treatments.

As the time for her daughter's new school year grew closer,

Joanne became a little sicker. By the time the school year began, her treatments had progressed and she started losing her hair. She spent a lot of time wondering if she should attend her daughter's school's PTA meetings looking the way she did with hardly any hair. She'd been very active in all the events that called for parent participation. She had friends among the other parents and she just didn't look the way she once had. She definitely didn't want people to stare at or feel sorry for her. But Joanne's greatest concern was for her daughter—she didn't want her to be embarrassed by having a mother with no hair. Besides these concerns, she didn't seem to have the same energy.

When it came time for the first PTA meeting, she wasn't sure if it was the right thing to do, but she went out and bought herself a wig. She'd had thick, shoulder-length hair and she couldn't find a wig that even remotely resembled it, but she did the best she could. She put that wig on and went to the meeting at her daughter's school. While most of the other parents were very kind to her, she couldn't help but notice some of them avoided her now. Others glanced furtively at her wig or gazed at her with nothing short of pity in their eyes. Joanne was so self-conscious she wanted to dash home, but she stuck out the meeting. Her daughter was in the classroom with all her peers, and Joanne couldn't bring herself to embarrass her any more than necessary by going to get her early, so she figured she'd wait until the meeting was over, slip into the back of the classroom when all the parents were collecting their children, and motion for her daughter to slip away with her.

When the PTA meeting ended, Joanne made her way to her daughter's classroom, careful to follow a small stream of other parents into the room. Prepared to silently signal for her daughter so they could slip out unobtrusively, Joanne was surprised when her daughter broke into a radiant smile, her eyes sparkling with adoration, and announced with pride, "That's my mom!" She ran to her mother's side and grabbed her hand and pulled her to the center of the room, introducing her to the teacher and to all of her friends without a trace of embarrassment or hesitation.

As they walked to the car, Joanne's daughter skipping beside her, still clasping her hand, told her, "Mom, you're the most beautiful mom in the whole school—in the whole world." Then she added, "You can wear the wig if you want to, but you don't have to. You're beautiful no matter what." Joanne looked at her daughter, surprised at how much someone so young could understand. Her daughter's complete sincerity shone from her eyes.

For some reason her daughter's uninhibited, loving reaction shifted Joanne's thinking. The risk her young daughter took in openly loving her in spite of her appearance gave her a new attitude about the risk involved in facing others when she looked the way she did. She found the courage inside herself to believe it was no longer necessary for her to hide or be embarrassed. She began to have faith inside herself—a faith that couldn't be placed on anyone or anything. Something shifted. See, with faith something shifts inside of us and we're not always clear what it is. We are not always able to articulate it, but a shift happens inside, and we're able to step up to a greater level of faith.

When it came time for the PTA to elect new officers, Joanne ran for office and won. What's more, she did so without the wig. She went to meetings with her head up and faced the world with dignity and assurance.

Her daughter never failed to shout with pride, "That's my mom. Look—my mommy's here!"

All of a sudden people came around and embraced her. No one avoided her or treated her with pity. It was because of a shift that took place in her—a shift that brought about the courage to risk, the courage to step out in faith, filing a whole new flight plan for dealing with the side effects of her treatment. She was no longer trying to hide something, but was instead able to embrace it.

Joanne's daughter has long since graduated and is married, and Joanne's a grandmother now. She experienced healing once she was able to embrace the truth of who she was, and to have the faith that she was okay, which may be tough sometimes. Just as it was tough for her to believe that her daughter's love could overcome embarrassment, it was tough for Joanne to have faith that she was a child of God. Just as her daughter was proudly saying, "That's my mommy!" Spirit was saying, "Yeah, that's my baby! That's where I am flowing." However, it was up to Joanne, just as it is up to each of us, to take the risk and to heal that sense of separation. She chose not to allow her illness and the side effects of its treatment to cause her to stall as she soared along the course of her grand flight plan as a mother and as a child of God.

When an airplane stalls, it's because there's too much pressure or force on the plane as it's ascending. What the pilot must do is to push the nose back down and regain the momentum; then the natural flow will stabilize the plane and return it to flight with a good attitude.

When you are willing to take a risk after you've stalled and stepped into the fear, and you then stand in the truth, you'll find the fear dissolves and the momentum returns. You'll find the sense of duality (of God and whatever else) begins to disappear. All that remains is God, and you're in the natural flow.

In our lives, when we know Spirit is there, when we know the essence of our being is love and know the truth of who we are, then we are willing to take greater risks. You've got to go beyond that point of those previous experiences you've labeled unlovable if you want to grow and expand in your world.

There's a fable about a land far away, whose sages set out to explore the regions far from their isolated jungle community to gather more wisdom and knowledge. Determined to expand their awareness and bring back more wisdom to their tribe, these sages filed a new flight plan, so to speak. Traveling through jungles, valleys and mountains, they searched for greater wisdom. Eventually from the top of a rolling hill they spotted the outskirts of a new city. Sitting on the horizon, there were skyscrapers—something they had never seen before—towering toward the heavens. The people of the city traveled inside, rather than on top of, strange animals with round legs. Winding their way along the hillside, they made their way to a place where long trails had been cleared. In awe, they watched as the people climbed into the bellies of huge birds that flew away with them, and they continued to watch as the birds disappeared from view. Initially, they wanted to approach and investigate all they saw before them. But one sage warned, "We should wait," catching the eye of another sage, who agreed, "Yes. Who knows what the risks are? Who knows what these things are?" A third sage nodded gravely, "They could explode." A fourth conceded, "Yes, or they could devour us. They could eat us if we don't know what they are." Again, the first sage, the oldest among them, spoke, "This is true. After all, there's great risk in the unknown."

So, all in agreement, they decided to sit down before approaching this new city of new sights—strange buildings, animals and birds—and figure out what they were. As they sat there and talked about what they could be, they drew upon their past experiences to figure it out. Using an old flight plan, they tried to determine their present location with an old map when they had been headed for an entirely new destination! They concluded the tall building absolutely had to have been put there with the help of some powerful and, no doubt, evil force. The animals these foreigners rode from place to place were obviously possessed of some wickedness as well. The gigantic birds had to be a treacherous trick of some sinister gods. After all, hadn't they viewed the people crawling in and out of their bellies to be flown away to who-knows-where? Too great a risk! So they headed back for their far-off village. They said, "Forget it!" They were very clear that what they had come upon was the way of evil; it was a dangerous place and they wanted nothing to do with it, so they didn't go there. Because of their belief—their thinking, their minds—they didn't follow their expanding hearts or their souls. They chose to follow the fear that came from a place in their own minds. They didn't allow the Light of the Spirit to shine the way, to reveal Itself with the blessings that a new experience can bring, an experience that would involve securing clearance for landing in a new territory, and then following the guidance given.

Sometimes, in the course of taking that risk, filing a new flight plan and soaring off in the unfamiliar, you may encounter turbulence. It could happen during any flight. Just because you face challenges doesn't mean it's time to bail out of the airplane. Keeping your parachute packed doesn't mean you have to jump out of the plane. It is the time to "keep the faith," focusing on the Light which dispels darkness, allowing you to see the course being set. Your new spiritual home is being built on God's time, on God's flight plan, because you have stopped fighting the forces trying to stall you and are going with the flow by surrendering to the Divine motion, Divine Light, Divine beacon, to that Divine Energy. When you have given away your will, when things unfold in a way contrary to how you thought they should, you can still look for God, knowing you will find the Spirit—that which is right.

God meets you where you are in life! Spirit, the Life Force, meets you where you are by eliminating the pressure against your wings and dipping into what is right for you. Just as you can feel It encouraging you toward great horizons and heights, It can bring the courage that you seek in your life. What is essential is to connect with the spiritual source, for right where you are, God is, and all is added unto. *All* is added—God is not withholding. It might look different. It may look like a mistake. But all is added. When I am able to be in this space, I am thankful Father/Mother God for this day, for this experience, for this breadth, for this life, for these friends, for this spiritual family. What we will find is we are beholders of the Divine in our lives in all areas—not just in some incidental places. With this knowledge, we will find an inner strength that will allow us to soar, going on to take risk after risk, filing new and greater flight plans for our expanding vision.

In retrospect, I'm sure a number of those mistakes or challenges in which you've found yourself, a number if the fears you've faced, the risks you've taken, have revealed their serendipitous reasoning to you. In Ernest Holmes' *The Voice Celestial,* when the Farer is going through this impatience, one of the lines the Voice shares is, "You cannot rush the harvest home." You cannot rush the harvest. The corn is going to be "corning" in its appropriate corn time. You are going to be experiencing, expanding, unfolding, growing and knowing in the appropriate time. You cannot rush the harvest home; you've got to learn to trust. When flying with Spirit toward ever-greater destinations, the estimated time of arrival is always: in God's time.

The Bible says, "Would God bring you to the point of birth and not deliver?" Would God bring you to that point of birth and not deliver? Of course not! The less resistance you have, the more the flow. That's so basic. Think about it. The less you resist the more Spirit flows, so if you give up the criticism, the condemnation, the skepticism, the fear and the cynicism—all these things that create resistance and create blocks for Spirit to get stuck on—the greater the flow. It seems so simple. Let's just get rid of the resistance in our lives. Let's give up the doubt and move into a courageous place of faith and action. The less resistance, the more It will flow into your life. Wow, that's simple. When we can keep it this simple, it's *powerful.*

Into Bondage

When you take risks and refuse to be bound to the old, familiar flight plan, and refuse to be bound by those limits some might say exist, you can catch the truth of yourself; you can remember it more and more. As you catch the truth of yourself, you will find such abundance and increased well-being that you'll be able to move through life growing, thriving and soaring.

As you stretch your ability to see a new and different way, a way in which the control tower with expanded vistas wants to guide you, it's up to you to make it welcome. You don't make it happen; that's the "how-to" stuff. But are you making the Spirit welcome in your life? Are you giving those opportunities for something greater to be experienced a place to show up? Are you so afraid of risk that you want to stay white-knuckled at the controls so you know you won't stray into any unfamiliar territory? God doesn't file a plan or place these aspirations in us without giving us the ability to bring them about; God doesn't give you the inspiration and vision without also providing the ability to create the reality—without supplying the flight plan on how to get there.

I'd like to end with some words that Nelson Mandela, quoting Marianne Williamson, said in his 1994 inaugural speech:

> *Our deepest fear is not that we are inadequate. Our deepest fear is that we are powerful beyond measure. It is our light, not our darkness, that most frightens us. We ask ourselves, "Who am I to be brilliant, gorgeous, talented, famous, fabulous? Actually, who are you not to be? You're a child of God. Your playing small does not serve this world. There is nothing enlightening about shrinking so that other people won't feel unsure around you. We were born to make manifest the glory of God that is within us. It is not just in some of us. It is in everyone and as we let our light shine, we unconsciously give other people permission to do the same, and as we are liberated from our own fear, our presence automatically liberates others.*

Liberate yourself from your fears, and you'll find you are liberating others to do the same. Take the risk—file the new flight plan you are inspired by Spirit to file and fly!

CHAPTER THREE

ENJOY YOUR FLIGHT

Spirit's power is most apparent
expressing through us
when we're living joyful lives.
Rather than seeking a brilliant career,
seek the brilliance within yourself.
When you recognize this brilliance,
it is released into expression.
Do what brings you joy,
what you love to do.
Go to work to express Spirit,
to express joy!
There's no more powerful way to increase
your gifts than to share them.

While headed off for a long-awaited vacation, a friend of mine sat staring out the window of the airplane, drinking in the beauty of the sky. She was determined to enjoy each moment of her time away. Flocks of fluffy, white clouds floated about the brilliant, blue sky outside her window. She breathed in her sense of wonder and appreciation, then looked down at the patchwork colors and textures of the land below. As she settled back in her seat, her gaze still wandering over the panorama out the window, her eyes were suddenly arrested by the sight of the plane's heavy metal wings. "How does this thing stay up here?" she wondered, her heart rate picking up speed. Seized by a moment of panic, she looked at the ground so far below her. Then her eyes darted to the massive size of the cabin of the passenger plane. "It seems impossible!" she thought, a flurry of lead butterflies seeming to take flight within her stomach.

"It was ridiculous," she later laughed. "I went from total joy and wonder in my flight to sudden fear the very moment I tried to figure out how it was possible!"

We can change the frequency of our perceptions as swiftly as the pilot can change the dials on her radios. When my friend told me of her experience, I was reminded of a story about three guys who were sentenced to execution by guillotine. One was a minister, one was a doctor, and one was an engineer. The minister was to be the first one executed. He was asked by the executioner, "Do you want your head down or do you want your head up?" The minister answered, "I'll look up." He put his head in the choke, and the executioner pulled the blade. The blade came down and stopped just before it hit the minister's neck. The king, who was there to witness the executions, declared, "Divine intervention! This man must be let go—let him go!" Overjoyed, the minister got up and left, a free man. Next, the doctor approached the guillotine. The executioner asked, "Do you want to face up or do you want to face down?" The doctor answered, "I will look up." He put his head in place and the executioner pulled the blade. The blade came down and froze just before it reached the doctor. "Divine intervention!" the king again announced. "He must be pardoned; let him go." Finally the engineer walked up to the guillotine and was asked whether he wanted to look up or down. "I want to look up," he replied, placing his head in the guillotine.

The executioner was preparing to pull the blade when the engineer said, "Wait, wait a minute; I see the problem."

Some people just have the engineering, analytical mind that wants to figure out—wants to know how! Rather than revel in the joy of their flight, the glory of God, the gifts of Spirit, they want to know how it's going to happen, how it's going to work. When we're reveling in the joy of flying we are looking at God, realizing the Presence, enjoying the splendor of life itself. Rather than trying to figure out how our flight is possible—how our life is going to work or unfold in the future—we are living to the present moment and experiencing the beauty of it.

Helen Keller said, "The best and most beautiful things of this world cannot be seen or even touched. They can only be felt." Spirit resides in this feeling place of our being. When we can get out of the analytical, engineering kind of mind, which is always trying to figure things out, then we are able to abide in this place of feeling. Of course there are appropriate places for the analytical mind. I'm not suggesting otherwise. We simply shouldn't allow it to take away from our joy in life or beauty in the present moment. Living is not about tiptoeing through life just to make it to death safely.

Divine Winds

Howard Thurman said, "A man without God is like a seed upon the winds." You know a seed has a life; it has the potential to be, and yet, caught upon the winds, it's just out there tossed about by the currents, floating around not knowing where it's going to land. If you are with God, you are like a seed with its potential upon the Divine wind, trusting you will be delivered to the appropriate place or field—to the appropriate relationship or to the appropriate deals or resolutions to whatever it is you are working on. It's up to you to take the time to make the connection and know Spirit, knowing God as your very life. Then it doesn't matter where you are.

A young guy named Harry Day had just graduated from high school and was about to go to college when his father died. Instead of going to college, he had to take care of the family's ranch in New Mexico. An old adobe building, the ranch house had no electricity or running water, and the ranch land covered many acres. Though working the land was hard, he made the best of it. Soon Harry met a woman, fell in love and married her. They had a baby girl, who was delivered at the nearest hospital, 200 miles away in El Paso. Since there was no school near the ranch for their daughter, Sandra, to attend, Harry and his wife homeschooled her. Wanting the best for her, when she grew older they sent her off to the best boarding school they could afford. The young girl and her family had determination. Finally she went off to college—Stanford, which was her father's dream. In 1952, she graduated with a law degree. At the time, the best offer she had, even with her law degree, was a position as legal secretary, so she went off to be a legal assistant in San Mateo. Later she moved to Arizona with her husband. Twenty-nine years after she began her law practice, the Attorney General for President Reagan called Sandra Day O'Connor and asked her if she would become the first woman on the Supreme Court.

You've got to trust Spirit and where It puts you down. It seems logical to enjoy the process you find yourself in, as opposed to being miserable. Spirit's currents of wind will put you down where you belong; enjoy the journey, the flight. The connection with your Source, the Life Force, makes the difference. It doesn't matter where you live or what family you were brought up in. Your history doesn't matter. Allow your destiny to supersede it. Experience the joy of your flight; revel in the awe of Spirit because you are a miraculous, unduplicated, superb individual. There are not two like you. Revel in the unique expression of Spirit known as you. Come to know it, because when we learn to live in the sense of feeling Spirit, we experience the miracles of life. Hear the conversation God is having with Itself through you.

Have you ever noticed how we become so busy we don't take the time to experience the joy of our flight? We're so busy we don't find time to revel in Spirit and reflect upon It. We're busy-aholics, or workaholics, or plan-aholics, running around so much we don't make the time to be with ourselves. If we have a moment at home, we just turn on the TV or stereo for background noise. (I know I have sometimes. On occasion, I've even been known to slip off to sleep at night with the TV going.) So the mind doesn't have a place of quiet or stillness. Here's another one: I've known people who just continue to read and read as opposed to simply taking time to be with their own minds and consciousnesses. I know reading is a wonderful thing (you're doing it now), but not at the expense of taking the time to revel in the Spirit tapping at the cabin door of your soul. Try telling yourself that you are wonderful—splendid. The down time is essential for replenishing our connections so that they remain clear. It's not uncommon to have one's pager buzzing, while talking on the cellular phone, while receiving a fax and having your e-mail ding with the latest message.

It takes time to fly with God, to know Spirit, to know what It sounds and feels like in your world—Its own unique interpretation through your own intuition. Did you take the time to watch the sunset yesterday? If you're in the middle of work, the work will wait, but the sun won't wait for you to finish what you're doing before it sets. *God is expressing.* Your work, your doing and your busy-ness will wait for you to take the time to come to know Spirit. Right around every corner there is a grand adventure. Right around the block there is something special—Spirit seeking to express Itself in your life, in your world. In the busy-ness, the running around, those activities we "have to do," sometimes we take on so many projects we don't do any of them well. Do you ever wonder, "Why did I say yes to another project?" This doesn't allow you much time to revel in Spirit and enjoy your flight. Instead, you end up wanting more time to be in your head in order to complete the project, the busy-ness of doing. We are just so busy *doing* and not *being.*

There's an old country saying: "Don't try to catch two frogs with one hand." I get a kick out of that one; for me it's so graphic. We try to do so many things. Instead we can revel in the joy of the flight we're on, in the splendor of Spirit expressing, which is ever present.

Have you ever seen those guys in the circus who get a plate spinning on top of a pole? First they get one plate spinning, then another plate and another. At first it seems easy, then all of a sudden it's comical, with them running back and forth trying to keep it all going. Sometimes we look just like that when we accept all those projects in our lives. Slow down! Enjoy the music. Enjoy the day. Enjoy the Spirit. Take time to reflect. That's where Spirit is—in the time of reflection and in the place where we are quiet.

To experience greater good in life, we must stop the busy-ness and doing-ness and take the time to revel in our flight with Spirit. Doing this we'll see and experience our flight at a level beyond our physical sight and touch. As Helen Keller told us, this is a sense of feeling. Many times the only feelings people get into are their fears. Fear constricts the mind, shrinking the periphery. Focusing on the challenges of the flight, rather than the good, the joy, the answers and solutions, those fears diminish the power of the mind. In order to avoid entering such treacherous flight conditions, take the time to revel in Spirit and to feel the joy of flying—of being.

When I came home the other night, Kalli was babysitting our little eight-month-old godchild, Savanna. You talk about a beautiful expression of love and joy. I love children; I just don't know what to do with them. There's nothing I can do to make a little eight-month-old happy if she decides not to be happy. But this little Light Being, this wonderful Spiritual Soul taught me to just be—just lie down and let her climb all over me and make faces and get me all sticky with whatever strange goo she had on her face and hands. It was just about *being* there with this child. It's not about forcing her to be happy, grasping for ways to do so. There's a Zen saying: "How do I grasp it? By not grasping. It's what remains after the grasping that is the true Self." It's about *being*. This little baby had a way of captivating the Presence. A child has a way of captivating the attention of a room. It's absolutely fully present. If you've ever been in a room with a little child, where is the attention? Right on the child! It's not self-conscious and it is able to entertain almost everybody who is looking at it simply by being. That's what the joy of flying is about. It is about *being* and coming to discover that who you are is just fine, appropriate and perfect for what's before you.

Joy in the Vicinity of Work

Some might say, "It's all very good to talk about the joy of 'being' rather than 'doing,' but I have to make a living!" Some of them even go to work each day hating to face the work they have to do—exhausted at the mere thought of spending a third of a day dreading the time. But when our energy flows toward co-creation with an inexhaustible Life Force, toward expressing Spirit in our work, it bubbles forth from deep within, renewing us throughout our day.

Your career can be an exciting flight course for you to savor each day. Success is knowing your talents and abilities are being used to express God. A successful career is not separate from your flight; it's part of the journey, and an extension of the unique child of God you are.

Rumi, the 13th-century Persian mystic, said, "Let the beauty of what you love be what you do." If you're going through life just working on trying to make ends meet or to acquire, going to work and stressing out, you're obviously not letting the beauty of what you love be what you do. In life *we make a living* by what we get, but we *make a life* by what we give. When you are doing what you love, you're giving of yourself; you're sharing yourself. Doing this you'll find the satisfaction you desire. Rewards aren't received because they're coming from things in life, but because you experience the richness inside you. When you're following your joy, your passion, doing the things you love, you're flying currents of joyful spirituality, which move through you with power. It is the currents of Source moving through you, carrying you joyously through this thing called life. You'll find yourself revitalized, energized and wanting to work late into the night because you love being what you are doing.

Sometimes near the end of a school year when I've been teaching four nights a week, going from eight in the morning to ten at night, I get tired and think, "Do I really want to teach?" Then I'll answer, "Of course I want to teach!" I step into the class and I start teaching. As I start speaking the words or facilitating the class, I find all of a sudden I'm recharged—revitalized. I've got this energy flowing through me. I come home and I'm awake, alive and enthusiastic. I started class at six-thirty that night tired and found that as the night progressed, I started getting into it; I experienced a surge of energy. The point is: You cannot be miserable and happy at the same time. You cannot be depleted and filled at the same time. Which one do you want to experience? Reflect upon that! You can have it. You can be that. It's not about grasping. It's not about making it happen. I don't try to make this happen.

If you're not finding any joy in your work, perhaps the work isn't right for you. Then again, perhaps your attitude simply needs to be corrected. We're not deciding what work that might be; rather, we're asking Spirit to reveal to us where It would have us go and what It would have us do. If you're talented at decorating, the talent is Spirit expressing. If something gives you joy, it's Spirit's way of telling you to go for it. There are some who are afraid if they turn it over to God, Spirit would have them doing something they don't like. Spirit is not going to have you go off and be an accountant if you don't like math. Life honors Itself as you. Give the joy of Spirit an opportunity to express as you.

Recently Kalli and I sat down to dinner at a vegetarian restaurant. There was a young waitress working there who walked around singing. I'll confess, at first I simply thought this was rather interesting. She bustled around, clearing tables, carrying trays, all the while singing these wonderful opera songs. When she took our order, she asked Kalli, "What can I get for you, milady?" Her obvious joy as she shared her passion and talent right where she was soon became my joy as well. This is how joy works; others are caught up in its glorious currents when it's expressed and shared. We were so moved that the tip we left for the joy she shared equaled half our check.

Spirit's power is most apparent expressing through us when we're living joyful lives. Rather than seeking a brilliant career, seek the brilliance within yourself. When you recognize this brilliance, it is released into expression. Do what brings you joy, what you love to do. Go to work to express Spirit, to express joy! There's no more powerful way to increase your gifts than to share them. Some of us are teachers, some are mechanics, some are accountants, some are doctors, some are street-sweepers, but we all have the same career—to express Spirit as who we are.

Inward Journey

Every journey she took, and they spanned her lifetime, was a quest to find a home in a place where she could dance every day with the wind. Through the years, she visited desert sand dunes, where the sands flew up to spray her steps, and she danced with the warm, dry winds. She visited seashores, where brisk, salt-laden breezes twirled her about with their own special song. On mountaintops and in distant countries, she danced with her wind, each performance choreographed by her soul. She whirled and flowed, all her senses alive with the vividness of being, and she felt completely at one, oblivious to all temporal. Always she sought out her lifelong dance partner—the wind. She sought out its music, its song—her lifelong love. She sought out freedom of her dance, and she searched for her home, where she could dance every day with the wind. But when the wind went away for days on end, she'd always decide it was time to move on. Finally she discovered the most wonderful thing: Every breath she drew was a bit of wind. She breathed it in and then out to life; each breath was a dance with her own wind. She learned when the wind stilled, the stillness was a part of the choreography; the stillness was a part of the rhythm, a pause between each changing note of the song. Sometimes we run around chasing the wind, chasing the joy of our dance, believing it's somewhere "out there," when in reality it's within us all the time. We need only remain open to its presence. This joy can be experienced when we're engaged in even the most mundane tasks.

A number of us from Seaside participated in a fabulous experience with a local chapter of Habitat for Humanity, helping with a building project. The community donated the land and other people in town donated the lumber, materials and labor. Some of the volunteers were outside in the hot sun painting, the paint dripping all over their faces, while I was inside muddying the drywall. A lot of us had more plaster in our hair than on the walls, and the messiness was wonderful. The joy of this great sense of community was a powerful experience. To be able to work with the couple who would own the home felt good inside.

I was talking to the gentleman who had donated the drywall and he said his weekly payroll runs around 50,000 dollars. I said, "Wow, it's nice to see how you are giving and life gives back to you." He said, "Oh, that's not why I'm giving. It's because what I feel inside is so wonderful only the great Father could give that feeling to me." This sense of feeling is Spirit. You can come to know It. You don't have to give to Habitat for Humanity. What you must begin to do, or do in a greater way, is take the inward journey. You'll come to discover those kinds of feelings—the sense and wonder—are there for you to experience. It's natural and right for you to feel this kind of joy. It doesn't have to be just a special moment in your week or in your life; it's something you can have all the time—when you take the time to reflect, to touch the Spirit.

If you are willing to take the inward journey, it doesn't matter if you are building a house, a town or a clubhouse for your kids. One is not any larger than the other to the Divine Intelligence that guides the universe. It can guide you in the creation of your business or the creation of your relationships. However, you must know the Spirit within, which will perfect that which concerns you. You're the one who has to stop giving your power away to outside forces. Remember the Zen saying: "It's what remains after the grasping, that is the true Self." You'll find what remains is God. What you'll find there is the love. What you'll find there is the joy, the possibilities, the magnificence—your true self. Sometimes we get caught up on the outside. If there is something that seems bigger and more demanding than your present capabilities, it's your mind's perception. It's time for you to come to know the truth and let go of the worry.

Stoned

Have you ever tried chewing chips and whistling at the same time? It's kind of tough. Well, we cannot live in a place of joyful love and trust, and live in fear and worry. You can't eat chips and whistle and you can't feel joyous love while being in fear. You get to choose one. What course do you want to fly? Which one do you want to come to know? If you want to begin to shift into a place of harmonious living, the choice is yours. Begin to take joyous flight on your inward journey.

There is a belief in the Hawaiian philosophy: A child comes into this world as a bowl of bright, shining light. As he begins to grow, rocks are put into this bowl and they tamper with the light—rocks developed through anxiety, fear, bitterness, jealousy, and thoughts of inadequacy and unworthiness. The bowl becomes heavier and heavier. So in our spiritual work, at least in the Huna philosophy, it's not about going out and finding enlightenment. It's about taking the inner walk and removing those stones that have gathered in the bowl, allowing the light already at the center of our being to shine. We came into this world just fine; then we began to *de*fine ourselves. Now it's time to *re*fine. The purpose is to bring forth the Presence into our lives—recognizing the Spirit of God as the Presence. We're told the Kingdom is within us. How do you find the Kingdom? You take off in flight to the inner self, enjoying the inward journey! No one can push your throttle forward for you; no one can make the choice for you. It's your choice. Are you tired of feeling as if the demands of this world are too big and you have too little joy in your life? Then it's time to reflect upon the "All Power" that needs you as the conduit of Its expression.

What Are You Seeking?

I want you to reflect upon this: "Am I seeking God, or am I seeking something from God? Am I seeking God, trying to find joy? Am I trying to find wealth? Am I trying to have a relationship work out the way I think it should? Am I trying to have this business transaction unfold the way I think it should? Am I trying to...?" Are you seeking God, or are you seeking something from God? Work with this one and you will find it will take you to an amazing place. Seeking God for the sake of seeking God will lift you to a higher altitude, and the joy and good are revealed.

How do you know if the Presence of God is dwelling in your consciousness? You come to notice there's a sense of joy, or there doesn't seem to be as much animosity in you. You're driving along the freeway and you're perfectly happy to let people cut in front of you. You begin to realize you are living life a little bit easier, living in a harmonious way with the world. You're dealing with the big issues, trusting there is an answer—not running around all stressed out, but living in a joyous, harmonious flow. Just because there may be places in your world that are going wrong doesn't mean your life is going wrong.

As you fly along this inward journey, know that what gets revealed to you is Divine. If it looks less than Divine, it is an opportunity to help cleanse your path, your world or your thinking. Continually bring your mind to reflect upon the Presence, and the possibility and wonder. Be the conduit to see the Presence. Everything in this world may not be wonderful, but it's not because God isn't there. It is an opportunity to bring your consciousness, which has attracted goodness and wholeness before, to this place so it can magnetize itself to bring in a greater expression of life into your awareness. The purpose of our being (I know it is a bit presumptuous to claim to *know*, but...) is to be the place where Spirit expresses. The Kingdom is right where you are. Where you are physically is irrelevant in terms of coming to know God. It is the perfect, appropriate, Divine and holy place. As you take the time to reflect upon the Spirit, taking flight on your inward journey, you will find riches of joy and love, as well as spiritual harmony in all you do.

Kick Off the Boots

We are alive to celebrate Spirit. Take the time to reflect upon God. No beating around the bush trying to think, "Ah, it's kind of this, kind of that." We are going right to Source. We are going right to Spirit and reflecting upon the essence as It moves in our lives. It's said, "There is no future in the past."

Too often, people use the past while attempting to create their future joy and they are perpetuating what has been. Spirit looks to express in a greater way than what you've experienced in your life thus far. You've got to create the space.

One winter, when everyone here on the mainland was all bundled up in their winter clothes, I headed over to Hawaii. I flew across the Pacific, climbed off the plane and BOOM—humidity and warmth. It was almost 80 degrees. One notices this kind of weather. This young guy in front of me got so excited he kicked off his snow boots and said, "Heaven! I have made it. Here at last!" He threw his boots on the tarmac, pulled off his coat and was fully present. There was no going back for this guy. When a realization hits—BOOM—the healing and the joy happens; the demonstration is. You kick off the boots and throw away the coat; the old stuff from the past is no longer appropriate. You kick off the boots and throw off the coat; you just know.

When I get in my plane, I don't think I can fly; I know I can. When we can move beyond just speaking words and saying spiritual stuff, and have the realization just as clearly as stepping out of the plane and realizing it's warm—BOOM—healing and joy happens. Realization is demonstration. I want you to think about that: *Realization is demonstration.* Instantaneously. There was the effect, and the young guy getting off the plane knew. Instantaneously, when you realize God is the Power, the Allness of Spirit, is when you realize the inseparability, the Presence. When you realize the Power is here, *healing and joy* happen and you are able to fly beyond your previous limits. You are able to fly beyond the parameters in which you have previously sputtered along. There is no future joy in the past. You could try to drag it along, but your future doesn't lie with dragging along the past. It lies in flying beyond it.

I have a cat named Ernest. I'll give Ernest a piece of wheat toast and say, "Here you go." He'll sniff at it, do his "whisker thing" and look at me as if to say, "Why are you trying to give this to *me*? Give it to your bird, not me. I'm a cat." But I'll tell you, if you're eating a tuna melt, Ernest is your best friend. He's right there rubbing against your legs, trying to look really cute, and basically begging. It's beneath the dignity of cats to beg, but he sure comes close. If you give him a piece of the sandwich, it's amazing what he'll do. He'll pull the top piece of bread off and eat the tuna as if it's the best thing in the world, and maybe lick the mayonnaise and cheese a little bit. When he's all done, the bread will still be lying there. I think, "Boy, this cat knows how to discern; he goes only for what he likes. This cat realizes and recognizes his self-worth." He's not willing to participate in anything less than what he likes. His thinking doesn't tell him, "I'd deserve tuna if I were a better cat. I should take any crumbs I can get. I'm the wrong color and wrong size of cat."

We can begin to experience the joy of consciousness, as opposed to thinking, "Well, it's okay to belittle myself because my upbringing says it's not good to be bold; it's better to be humble," or whatever is in one's thinking. It's time to move beyond this. This past is what is holding you back from the joy of the glorious future of your dreams. You are capable of experiencing the fullness of joy in your life. Every decision you make—every decision, bar none—is a reflection of your consciousness. It's a reflection of what you think about yourself. If you think you are worthy, you'll be going out there and creating the gifts and joy that support this belief. There's something called pilot-controlled lighting, where you click your microphone seven times at night and you turn on the runway lights. There is no need to touch down in the dark, but you must remember to turn on the lights. Begin to relax, begin to breathe, take control of your mind and you'll begin to find a world reflecting your choices. We get so busy trying to grasp it, to understand it and put these metaphysical principles into practice when there's nothing to grab! If people study it and don't see it, they've approached it too eagerly. It's easy! It's a reflection. So often what we're attempting to do is to grasp it with our old model. We attempt to grasp it with our way of thinking. Slow down. Spirit will know when to push. Spirit's joy is pushing Itself through you. You don't have to do the pushing. Spirit knows how to fill you with joy. Life is not playing hide-and-seek or tag with you.

Have you ever lain outside at night when you were camping and looked up at the sky when the stars and moon were shining? Lying there all night in the dark, did you start to wonder when the sun was going to come back? Not that you were scared, but you were ready for the sun to finally shine. You'd been lying awake long enough. Wouldn't you know it? Up came the sun, as beautiful as it could be. Were you responsible for the sun's showing up? Of course not! The sun was going to rise anyway. Take a look at beautiful trees blossoming in all their green and the gorgeous flowers in all their colors. Are you responsible for those? Of course not! They are going to blossom. They are going to do their leaf-thing. That's their nature. Guess what? It's God's nature to express Itself, and It is going to continue to express Itself and find the open vector through which to express. We do not need to struggle. We do not need to grasp. We do not need to fight. We simply must choose to enjoy our flight.

Great Thoughts

Ernest Holmes said, "Great things are done by people who think great thoughts and then go out into the world and make their dreams come true." Where do these great thoughts come from? They come from within. They come from Spirit, and when we're willing to be open, we begin to know. But you have to create the space. If you want to experience a greater, grander, more joyful future, you begin RIGHT NOW by being in the Presence and realizing it. Too often our minds are preoccupied with the ways of this world, denying the conscious experience of the Presence. You will experience the values of your choices in life. You can honor the something inside of you, which is God, Spirit speaking, the inner voice—it's not the destructive, self-sabotaging mind chatter, which is trying to pull you down and keep you grounded and shackled to past ways of being. The Presence wants you to fly, to soar to new levels of joy. This presence is the One bringing the grand ideas, the strength, the way and the ability to reach those thoughts. You must have the courage to fly up there.

It's not by your efforts, or because you are forcing it. Spirit is with us always. What we do is realize the Presence and It lifts us up. It is about knowing the Presence in your life, every hour of every day, week, month and year. The joy is seeking to push Itself, to birth and to express Itself. All It needs is for you to call it forth, because the airspace is cleared for you to fly through and the way you fly through is to *realize*. Kick off those old boots, throw out the old coat, and just come to realize what is. In the realization is the demonstration, the joy and the magnificent expression of God. The expression of God feels good. It's peaceful. It's in this sense of love and joy that miracles happen. All the necessary resources are present. Spirit has implanted them, along with the ways and the means to get there.

Surprise of a Rainbow

The wisdom of a joyful heart begins with surprise. When you are afraid of disappointment, surprise is not welcome. It is the surprise of a rainbow. Intellectually we all know how rainbows happen, but all of a sudden to see it, to know the quickening of joy at the sight of the rainbow is beyond the intellect. The surprise of being touched by magical music—the wonder of experiencing it—this is where joy comes from. It comes from a willingness to trust life. It comes from a willingness to know you are a recipient of God's joy, for joy is an infallible sign of the presence of God, as Teilhard de Chardin tells us: "...from joy springs all creation, by joy it is sustained, toward joy it proceeds, to joy it returns."

Joy! It makes the heart sing. I truly believe joy is expressing, which means not just sitting around and doing nothing. As you listen to the news of the silence, it gives you the signs and guidance, bringing you a sense of fulfillment in activities that enliven your soul and being. So often people come up with a great Divine idea and then sit back and say, "God will provide." Know anybody like that? They do nothing. The saying is, "If you're looking for milk this would be about as good as sitting down in a field on a seat, waiting for a cow to back up to you."

In Religious Science we say, "Treat (our form of prayer) and move your feet." The English have a saying, "Pray devoutly and hammer softly." An Indian saying is, "Pray to God and row your boat away from the rocks." The ancient Greek playwright Sophocles, in the 400s BCE, said, "God cannot help the man who does not act." An ancient Chinese saying is, "He who waits for roast duck to fly into his mouth waits a very, very long time." God, Life, Spirit—I don't care what you call it—is calling, knocking upon your soul from all over, but activity on your part is essential. It is essential for you to reach out, to touch somebody, to take action and fly toward your dreams—your bliss.

Let go, take off, begin to live in the Presence, right here, right now, and experience the joy of your dreams as you revel in the joy of your flight.

WEATHERING STORMS & TURBULENCE

Praying to a concept of God
is no different than the pagans,
who used to pray to their idols,
which was a concept of God to them.
If we can begin to let go of our concepts
and structure, going to Spirit
and opening up, allowing ourselves
to be moved so we know
what steps to take and what words to say,
then we will be praying with our minds,
our hearts, our souls and consciousness
in a very powerful, healing,
embracing way.

Almost every frequent flyer (to say nothing of pilots) has experienced some sort of turbulence or flown through at least one storm, if not many. Turbulence and storms can be frightening experiences; the plane is thrown off balance, and its occupants are shaken around and may not be able to see through the black clouds and driving rain. These things don't make for the smooth flight one hopes to enjoy. During our flight through life we usually have some spans of turbulence. After all, sometimes it's tough in life and there are going to be storms. The key is how you weather the storms.

Some time ago, I had a speaking engagement in Prescott, Arizona, on a Friday night and a wedding to perform back home in California the following morning. I hadn't yet earned my pilot's license, so David Kilbourne, a friend who is a pilot with many years of experience in the skies and the person who inspired me to fly, flew me there. We flew in his small experimental plane, a Very E-Z, which was even smaller than the Cessna-152 I was learning to fly in. On Friday we took off as a storm rolled in with winds howling off the ocean. Those currents of wind from the ocean at our back whooshed us to Arizona in less than an hour-and-a-half. The sky was so black and rainy we couldn't see the ground or the airport. With all the wind and pounding force of rain, there was a great amount of turbulence. Fortunately, inside the plane there are instruments. A pilot doesn't have to see what's outside the plane if he is able to trust the instruments inside. Dave knew just how to read and stay focused on them. Guided by the instruments, he brought us in and set us down on the slick runway for a perfect landing, and I was able to get to my workshop on time.

The next morning, we awoke and found the rain had turned to snowflakes. It was snowing in Prescott, Arizona! Arriving at the airport, Dave and I stood there looking up at the skies, which were growing blacker and darker, discussing whether we should go or wait. Waiting would mean I wouldn't get back in time for the wedding. If our well-being was at stake, missing the wedding would have been fine. However, with his experienced eye, Dave assessed the skies and pointed out a blue hole in the clouds. We chipped the ice off the wings and Dave flew the plane up toward the blue hole, circling higher and higher. The cloud moved in beneath us so we couldn't see the ground any longer. (I noticed the ground is a very comforting thing.) Cessnas usually fly at about 8,000 feet, but I watched as Dave took us to 10,000 feet, then to 11,000 feet, then to 12,000 feet. Surrounded by these mountains of clouds, we climbed higher and higher. Then we flew into these clouds. In the middle of such clouds you can lose all sense of direction. You don't know if you're up or down or sideways! Inside the plane there is something called the "attitude indicator," an instrument that can help you stay peaceful because it allows you to know whether or not you're in level flight when all your physical senses don't have a clue. When flying in the midst of clouds it's so important not to get caught up on the outside—to stay focused on those inner instruments.

When we're in a cloud or experiencing some turbulence in life, feeling as if we don't know what's going on, we can sometimes get caught up on the outer appearance. But if we remember to stay focused on those inner guides when fear creeps in, we don't have to do battle with the fear. A couple thousand years ago the Greek philosopher and poet Empedocles said, "Men are disturbed not by what happens to them, but by their opinion of what happens."

Staying focused on our inner guide and not getting lost on the outer perceptions keep us in level flight. Staying unopinionated during flight, one realizes doing combat with fear is a waste of energy better spent focusing on the truth. Ego says to the mind, "Believe in this fear! Forget about God and believe in this fear!" When we get into fear, into worry, we want to control. As we work on gaining greater control—of our health, our life, our relationships, our finances—we say, "Hey, God, it's my will! Back off until I get things lined up, then you can step in!" Before the moment of fear and anxiety weighs heavily on us we should let go and trust our inner instruments to guide us!

Dave trusted the plane's inner instruments and had us climbing out of the clouds at 15,000 feet. Sometimes we have to gain altitude to climb above clouds, mountains or blockages, like scaling new heights to view the problems in our lives from a less threatening angle. Still, this new dimension can be scary because we haven't flown there before. While these elevations may not be the ideal path for the journey, they may be a necessary leg of it. You lose oxygen at about 14,000 feet. This means your brain begins to lose oxygen. We were at 16,000 feet, climbing still to 17,000 feet—then 18,000 feet. It took us longer than an hour to climb this high. I figured we must be near home, when I heard over the radio, "Prescott, Arizona, cleared for landing." It took us almost as long to get up over the clouds as it took us to get to Arizona the day before. I said, "Hey, Dave, you ever climbed to 18,000 feet?" He replied, "Yeah—once."

When the brain reaches those altitudes where it begins to lose oxygen something called hypoxia happens. We didn't get to that point. (At least, I don't think we did.) Hypoxia slowly slips in and you fall asleep, which isn't good when you're flying. In our lives what can happen is spiritual hypoxia. Spirit, like oxygen, stops creeping into our minds and our awareness, and as with hypoxia, we go to sleep. It begins to slip into our lives at the point where we buy into the world—buy into the effects, into the bank account, into believing what the headlines say, into believing things aren't working in the world. Then, all of a sudden, we go numb; we go to sleep to our spiritual connection, believing the outside as opposed to those instruments within. Those inner instruments will guide us.

Dave, with his years of experience, guided by those inner instruments, took us out of the flight paths of the jumbo jets and brought us safely home.

Can You Remember in the Storm?

A country western song says, "Sometimes in life, you're the windshield and sometimes you're the bug." Even when we're walking with Spirit, in the Presence, those challenging times slip into one's thinking and mind. Let's be real—they do creep in. At one time or another even the greatest spiritual teachers have slipped into fear, if just for a moment. It's not as if "forever and ever, amen," we go out without questioning the decisions or the activities in our lives. One of the things that slip in is the fear, or the questioning or discontent, of the challenges in our world. The turbulence is a result of our carnal mind (our human or physical mind) believing in two powers instead of one. Finding the proper altitude through the turbulence in our flight comes as we unify with God. We must get rid of the duality involved in attempting to contact the Power—God—somewhere on the outside, and trust the power within, the autopilot that knows how to put us back into level flight.

To do this we must get beyond our concept of the way God is and the way God's supposed to be approached, and begin to open up to what is, because God is. Wherever you are, God is, on the ground or at 18,000 feet. If we can remember this right in the midst of any situations that arise, we will begin to experience a healing in our lives. It can be this simple, but actually putting it into practice in the midst of a storm is not always so simple.

Many times we go to Spirit because something doesn't feel right in our lives. Something's out of balance—something's bumping the plane around—such as the body being unhealthy. We know something isn't right because it doesn't feel right inside.

True? This means at the core of our being is the good, the whole and the completeness. Things don't seem right when we are away from this, so it's nice to be able to use this indicator to get our attitude back on course. Getting back on course means surrendering to the Essence, the Power, the Life Force, and allowing it to guide you.

Sometimes people do nothing more than repeat words when they pray because this is the way they were taught. What I have come to discover is praying in a rote manner, without seeking to connect with the heart, is no different than praying to a golden calf (which got the folks of Moses' time in trouble). If said without the heart, it's like saying, "This way is going to work," and believing, "This golden calf is going to deliver the goods." Praying to a *concept* of God is no different than the pagans, who used to pray to their idols, which was a concept of God to them. If we can begin to let go of our concepts and structure, going to Spirit and opening up, allowing ourselves to be moved so we know what steps to take and what words to say, then we will be praying with our minds, our hearts, our souls and consciousness in a very powerful, healing and embracing way.

There were two guys parachuting from a plane. Suddenly the wind currents kicked up and the gales began to whisk the men this way and that. The first guy panicked; he got into fear, worry and concern. Struggling against the wind, tugging with all his might on the cords of the parachute, he fought to keep them untangled. But because of the fear, the anxiety and worry that filled his mind as he struggled against the mighty air currents, the cords of his parachute became all the more tangled, until finally they threw the parachute off in such a way that the man plummeted to the earth. The second guy, realizing the power of the wind and air currents, let go, riding the currents and allowing them to carry him along in the turbulence. Finally he was dropped off in the safety of a field, which just happened to be where he wanted to land. In our lives, if we take time to walk with God and understand Spirit, and our world gets hit by turbulence, sweeping us up in these very strong currents and pulling us beyond our ability to control the flow of life, it is easier to stop fighting it and begin to trust God. Trust the turbulent flow taking you in the direction your life is intended to go.

Getting Quiet

It takes time to be able to live with this kind of trust. This is why you take time daily to meditate. Often you are sitting there in meditation and you don't necessarily get much at that moment. You don't necessarily get instant gratification from your meditation. Yet, after days, weeks, months or years of practicing this "bliss-ipline," when you find yourself sucked into the vortex of some stormy turbulence which appears to be out of your control, rather than drawing upon what's usually thought of as a natural human instinct of flight, fight, faint or freeze, you pull from your deeper subjective of the months, weeks and years of spiritual work. Then, instead of panicking, you are able to trust Spirit to maneuver you to the perfect altitude. All the time you spent coming to understand Spirit serves you in those periods of challenge and turbulence when your life seems to be out of your control. Do you follow this? Do you *feel* the meaning of what I'm saying? This is the value of taking time, even when it feels like, "Boy, I could get a lot more done in those 20 minutes than if I just sat and experienced my oneness with God."

This oneness, this peace, is something we have to experience for ourselves. It's not something we can get vicariously. This concept sounds good, but can you really let go and trust the Presence? So many people go to God believing they have to pray to get Him to save them, as if God is withholding. People prostrate themselves or get down and beg God. If nothing really comes through right away, they start making deals with God, as if God could be withholding anything from us. God has already given it all. Life is all. This is why it's essential for us to take the time to come to realize the presence of God.

In the Bible, James wrote, "If you ask and you receive not, it's because you've prayed amiss." We're praying amiss when we're asking God for something, shutting off the infinite flow by our little minds being placed in duality, declaring separation and living in turbulence. If you can take the time to know God, then you'll find you know God or Life as your life, as your success, as your fulfillment, as your happiness. You'll find Spirit showing up in your world. The Intelligence that guides the universe is the same One operating in your life. The One that turns grass green is the same One working right there in the midst of turbulence, but you've got to trust. Trusting comes from doing your spiritual work, meditating and taking the time to connect with Spirit, to know It, to feel It, to sense It.

I've come to realize the importance of connecting with the Spirit in one's activities. Sometimes we just live in the world and forget to incorporate the Spirit into what we are doing, neglecting to check on our inner instruments. Before a pilot ever takes flight, he does a preflight check on the plane to assure all is well. When we are living in the awareness of Spirit as our center, we will have done our preflight check and will be ready for whatever comes our way. We are then able to remember Spirit is the mind, the body and the consciousness through all things. So often metaphysicians or New Age folks get so far off in the spiritual realm that we're living in an "airy-fairy" place. We set off on our flight without going over our flight plans. Balance matters; it is being able to be centered and maintain a smooth flight. This comes from taking time in our lives, in the midst of confusion, to breathe and remember God is here, even in the midst of the catastrophe or challenge, because there *is* an answer. You have checkpoints to keep you on course. When off course, you get to choose between fear and finding your way back. Now, are you going to come from a place of centeredness? Are you going to take the time and know there is an answer, or are you going to buy into turbulent energy in the atmosphere? When wounds from the past come forward in your life, do you feel angered by them, or do you choose to be kind to yourself? Do you allow those childhood memories to take flight and blow you off course, carrying you to places you don't want to go? Do you allow them to bring forth anger, or do you choose to accept, to forgive? How about times you have been violated in your life? Do you choose shame? Or do you choose to let go and move on with your life, to accept who you are? In times of fear and isolation, do you choose courage and strength in your life? See, the choice comes down to you and the consciousness in which you choose to make the decisions in your life. From time to time there is turbulence that will bounce you around. The situations in life are only bringing forth the lessons. You can take the time to look and see if there's a pattern emerging, pointing you on the wrong course. You can also choose how you're going to deal with your life. The degree of consciousness that emerges is up to you, because the fact remains that God is fully present.

Saint Augustine said, "God's center is everywhere and circumference nowhere." Whether saint of sinner, both are dealing in this field of consciousness, both are dealing in the realm of Spirit. Saints have just chosen to have a greater degree of awareness of

God, or the Father, or the Presence, or the Life Force. Sinners, those who are missing the mark, have chosen at that juncture in their lives to buy into their humanness, a humanness that senses separation. But the truth is that we're never really separated from God. It is only a sense of separation that allows us to operate in this realm of humanness.

Where Do You Dwell?

As we come to realize God's presence, if something does come up in our world and we lose what we're holding on to or valued, or saved for a rainy day, what comes to us is an opportunity to realize God has not left us. The Spirit created our good in the first place and hasn't gone anywhere. What we have is an opportunity for us to know God and not fear the turbulence, knowing we are not those things—we are not those savings and we are not dependent upon another person. When we are able to come from centeredness, from balanced flight, we cannot be thrown off course. We will feel the turbocharged center fire us to a whole new stratosphere of understanding. I don't care what the situation is, or how horrific—and I have heard some biggies (from my perspective, not God's)—I have watched people come back with their heads up. When they came upon the checkpoints in their flight, instead of choosing shame, they chose "forgivenness." Instead of choosing the anger or bitterness or despair, they reflected upon the presence of God showing up right there.

Ernest Holmes wrote:

> *Let us learn to be happy even in the midst of unhappiness, to laugh even in the midst of tears, to believe even in the midst of unbelief. The man who does this is one whose foundation is*

certain; he is the man who is able to look out into the world, and, letting his thought dwell on the invisible essence of Reality, say—and mean it—'Bless the Lord, O my soul: and all that is within me, bless his holy name.'

When we let our thoughts dwell in the invisible essence of Reality, we come to the realization that God isn't something we attain—the good is not something we go out to get. It's God who gave us the power to create it in the first place. It is this life-flow we can neither hold nor hoard. When we move into a place of realization, we experience the unfoldment of needs being met, not because we're trying to get it, but because it is the natural unfoldment. We are led to the people who are able to assist us; the right information brings the correct insights, because we are coming from a place of connection with Source. It's like the flower. When it opens up, the fragrance is released. When we are connecting with our Source and coming to a more conscious state, the success, the fulfillment, the attainment comes—not because that's what we're after, but because it's the natural unfoldment when we're coming from centeredness.

There's an often-told story of a young rabbi in a small village, who felt he was very wise. People didn't quite recognize this in him, but he felt he was. He was clever; that's one of the things few people would argue. One day, an old, wise rabbi, who was touring the region, was coming through the young rabbi's town. This young guy wanted to prove himself, so he thought, "Maybe I'll try to trick this old rabbi. What I'll do is grab a little bird. I'll hold the bird in my hand and go to this rabbi and say, 'Oh, wise one, the bird I hold in my hand, is it alive or is it dead?' If he says it's alive, it will be easy enough to squish it and show him that it's dead. But if he says it's dead, I will just open up my hand and let it fly away."

The next day when the crowd gathered and the time seemed right, the young, aspiring rabbi got up and walked to the middle of the crowd. Holding up his hand, he said, "Oh, wise teacher, is the bird in my hand alive or dead?" The crowd "oohed" in wonder of what was going on. The wise rabbi just paused for a moment and said, "It's up to you."

This is what Spirit says to us about our lives: "It's up to you. You can destroy it. You can squish it. You can kill it, or you can live. You can fly." The wise, loving presence of the Spirit allows you to choose the way you respond to those things that go on in your life. You may come from a place of centeredness and connectedness and reflection—knowing there is Spirit here—or you can buy into the humanness, the fear and the turbulence. You're at the checkpoint, and when you are at the checkpoint within your life, you always get to choose. Are you going to choose Spirit?

People often say to me, "Of course I'm going to choose Spirit, but I just have to get rid of this pain in my life first. If my body just didn't ache, then I would be more comfortable and I would have time to pursue Spirit. You know, Christian, as soon as I'm able to pay my rent, when I'm not worried and I can be at a greater level of peace, then I'll be able to find Spirit...have this money or this relationship, then I will be..." The list goes on and on, as if Spirit is dependent upon some physical proof. We cannot change some human disorder for human harmony, because what we are doing is dealing in the physical realm. But if we choose to go to God, if we take the time to reflect upon the Presence in our lives, we're going to find it unfolding like the flower releasing its fragrance. Our world will begin to release greater beauty, greater love and greater well-being. We'll have laughter even in the midst of tears, believe even in the midst of unbelief and find calm in the midst of turbulence.

I've been asked if there are any shortcuts. There is one shortcut: to pull those fears out of one's thinking consciousness, and put your heart and your soul on looking at Spirit, on realizing the Presence in all things, not on the attainment but on the Divine realization—the invisible essence of Reality. That's the shortcut; you drop all the garbage and allow your heart and soul to reflect upon Spirit. Simple!

God meets us where we are in our lives, no matter the turbulence. Spirit, the Life Force, meets us where we are and can bring the comfort we seek in our lives. We are told God is our comforter—we will not be left comfortless. Spirit meets us where we are. It's essential for us to connect with the spiritual source, for right where I am, God is, and all is added unto. All is added—God is not withholding. It might look different. It may look like a mistake. But all is added unto us. When I'm able to be in this place, I am thankful Father/Mother God for this day, this experience, this life, these friends and this lesson. We will find we are the beholders of the Divine in our lives in all areas—not just some sacred places, but in the most difficult circumstances and turbulent predicaments in which we find ourselves. We will find an inner strength that will allow us to stand and speak the spiritual truth. When it gets dark, hazy and cloudy outside, trust the inner instruments.

Food for Flight

A man came up to me once and said, "It seems like ministers believe what they have to say on Sundays is so important. I know all of you take a lot of time preparing your sermons. Well, I've been coming to church for a couple years now and I've probably heard about a hundred of your sermons. You know what? I can't remember one single sermon. In fact, I can't even remember one line. It makes me wonder if my time wouldn't have been better spent somewhere else."

Smiling at the guy, I replied, "I have been married for many years. During that time I have eaten thousands of meals, most of them prepared for me by my wife, Kalli. Thinking about it now, I can't remember the menu of a single meal. But I'm certain if I hadn't eaten them I would have starved to death."

If we can continue to feed our souls, to nurture our bodies, to stimulate our minds—if we can continue to just do this in a very simple way—we're going to find we're able to remain at peace in the midst of those episodes of turbulence. We're going to find we're able to know the truth in the midst of heated conversation. We're going to be able to know the Presence because we will have taken the time to feed our hearts and souls, and to know the Spirit for what It truly is. It will be very simple to keep our center of gravity.

Be in the moment and recognize if you're fighting the power of any turbulence by telling yourself, "Don't think that, think this," then there is duality going on. There is competition. Remember: To know God is the only Power. One of the very simple things we can do is to focus our minds on a singular thought, and allow the natural guiding system to steer us through.

The actor James Earl Jones, with his great voice, his portrayal of Darth Vader and the many other roles he's played, stuttered as a child until he was 14 years old. He overcame those times of turbulence. He did not believe in the boundaries. The boundaries the mind gives you are unreal, yet your vivid imagination believes in them.

Stephen Hawking, one of the greatest minds of our day, the theoretical physicist who has transformed our view of the world, and who wrote *A Brief History of Time,* has Lou Gehrig's Disease. He can hardly speak, yet he still lectures and writes books by holding a little wand in his mouth, bringing forth amazing details to us.

Tom Dempsey, the football player who kicked the longest field goal in a playoff game, had no toes. These people refused to buy into those false boundaries of the mind, which could create turbulent doubts. You are the one who has to have the courage to fly through those skies that look so ominous. Once you've flown in, you're with the flow of this jet stream. It's moving you. It's not like you've got to do it all, but you've got to have the courage to fly into the all-ness of it.

Mother Theresa said that when she looked into the eyes of the dirty, sick, dying children of Calcutta, she saw the face of God. Wow! Talk about some physical and emotional turbulence not seen! Instead of turbulence, in the midst of the dying she was able to see the face of God. Are you able to look into those painful, tough situations in your life and see the face of God? It's up to you to look for God in those tough places. You're the one who has to have the courage not to believe when your mind and physical senses are telling you, "This is bad." It may not be a good situation, but it's important to know that, even if you missed the checkpoint, God is still there.

In Joshua it says, "Be not afraid, neither be dismayed, for the Lord God is with you wherever you go." If you are in darkness, in times when your flight seems to be thrashing you about and dropping thousands of feet with every jolt, know Spirit, your copilot, is there. As you recognize the Spirit, It will lead, bringing forth peace and new ideas.

Spirit's There

There's an old Indian proverb: "Call to God, and row your boat away from the rocks." Call to God; go to Spirit and recognize It. Then do what It directs you to do—what is right, what is healthy and what is whole. In the world in which we live fear is often used to guide us. Children are raised with fear: "If you do that, you're going to get smacked." Using fear as a guide, instead of peace and love, we teach people the value of separation and isolation rather than of unity and wholeness. We are a bundle of boundaries. We've got these myths in our minds creating chasms, creating the separation. Allow the Spirit and the presence to move in your life. If you knew the presence of God flew with you, you would fear nothing; you could fly through the valley of the shadow of death and fear no evil.

If you take your problem to prayer, the problem enters into your prayer. This is the way we've been taught: "I am now praying for this problem. Instead, begin to allow a shift to take place in mind. What we want is to know the truth. If there's a problem or a challenge going on in your world, often people want to know the truth of the problem. They want to know the truth of the condition, situation or person. There is only one truth—this truth is God! If you've got a condition you want to take into prayer, I want you to stop taking it into prayer and begin to know the truth—the only truth there is—God, Spirit, this Life Force, this Energy that animates us. In prayer, remember to know God, not your problem, not the truth about your problem, but to know the presence of God lifts you above any turbulence to an altitude where there is calm.

In Isaiah it says, "God will keep him in perfect peace, whose mind is staid on Him." I want you to do this prayer work. It's easy to allow the mind to go toward the turbulent condition. This is high spiritual stuff being written here, and it's very simple. When we keep our minds on God, we will experience the peace; then we will experience the truth. Spirit knows how to take care of the situation; I don't need to tell God how to heal. I don't need to tell God how to take care of my bank account. I keep my mind on Spirit and know the truth. Then I'm able to experience peace in my life. My place is to recognize the presence of God right here, no matter the appearance of turbulence or stormy conditions. Somebody calls you with some indigestion; it's about knowing God knows how to heal. Somebody calls you with trouble at work; the position is to know God is the employer and the employee. It's not to find the person a job. It's not about convincing the person's consciousness there is a perfect place of employment. It's about knowing Spirit. It is recognizing the presence in the midst of everything. This is when healing happens.

People say, "But Christian, what about this?"

I say, "Yeah, and where is God there?"

People say, "But look at this."

I say, "Yeah, and where's God?"

"But don't you understand?"

"I do. And where is God there?"

You don't have the power, and prayer is not the power—the power is God. So the first step to powerful prayer is the recognition of Spirit.

Another one I've heard is, "You know, my life used to really work. I had this nice relationship (or house or job). My world these days is just so much more of a struggle. It's tough. I lost it all..." Have you ever heard anybody run this story? Do you really think God would be giving you good one moment and withholding at another? Of course not! All good is present, right here, and it is a matter of our recognizing it. People have learned to manipulate the power with mind over matter, using their own energy, which eventually wears out. Let Spirit's energy run through you, guiding you, and experience the lasting power of the presence.

Do you think lighting candles and staying up all night to pray really makes a difference to God? Of course not. But if you're moved to light candles and stay up all night in prayer (Lord knows I've done that before), then do it because it's how Spirit is interpreting Itself through you, assisting you to have a shift in mind, assisting you to become pure and clear. Although it's okay, the rituals you perform aren't what matter. Of themselves, they don't mean anything to God. God is fully present, assisting you. What matters is the shift of your awareness.

There is a wonderful quote from Ernest Holmes:

> Since some people have been healed through prayer, while others have not, the answer is not that God has responded to some and not to others, but that some have responded to God more than others. The answer to prayer is in the 'prayer'.

The answer to your prayer is in the one praying. It's not in God. God is not keeping anything from you. It is up to us to recognize the Presence is fully present; no matter what decision you have to make in your life, the Spirit is moving you. The military will fly some of their planes right into the center of a hurricane and they will come through undamaged. Spirit is infinitely greater than the military. You have what it takes to fly right into the center of the worst of conditions and come through having learned what it's all about.

When I talk about challenges, I'm not saying they're bad. I'm talking about opportunities that make you stretch. Someone once said, "Those who have a dozen challenges are twice blessed than those who have half a dozen challenges." Those times of challenge or turbulence are making you stretch in your life, inspiring you to call upon Spirit and recognize Spirit in those times and places—those opportunities.

If faced with turbulence in making a decision, let us allow the Spirit to shine through us. Let us remember to fly with God and allow God to move you. I don't really think there is a right decision and a wrong decision. There is a God decision moving through you, assisting you to see God in all things. Allow your life to be your message.

There's a cute story we tell in our Junior Church about a new angel who went to Heaven. A senior angel of angels said to him, "Hey, you've got an assignment. I want you to go out and find one of the most powerful prayers on Earth." So the new angel took his assignment and went out looking. His first stop was all the churches and temples and synagogues, but he couldn't really find what he was looking for there. When he finally returned, he had a little boy with him. The senior angel said, "You returned with a little boy? What's up?"

To which the new angel answered, "Well, I went to all these great temples and houses of worship. I listened to men and women repeating phrases and statements that just boggled my mind with how brilliant they were, yet in their hearts they didn't really understand the words themselves. I went to other places where they uttered delicate poetry and psalms and words—and yet, it was hypocrisy. They didn't really get it. So I was coming back, because I knew you'd be wondering where I was, and as I was coming over the busy city, I heard a little boy crying. I went down to the little boy and as I listened closer, I heard him saying the alphabet. He was saying, 'A, B, C...' and as I listened closer, I could hear him talking to God, saying, 'God, I don't know how to read, and I don't know how to do any prayers, so the prayer books don't do me any good. But I thought if I gave you all the letters, you could just put it together the way you like it.'"

That's the connection we're looking for—realizing the Presence of God is here and trusting It to put it all together. Our responsibility is to realize God, not some anthropomorphic being who's in a foul mood, throwing lightning bolts as He sits in judgment of you. That concept of God went out with Zeus and Apollo. We're dealing with a Life Force—a Presence in which we live and move and have our being. We are dealing with a Presence that is here. We're not out there attempting to go to God on our own or on someone else's behalf to get something done. This concept just doesn't fit with the intellectual and heartfelt beings of today. It is time to realize, as we travel with Spirit, exactly who we are. Who are you? In the silent realization of your being, you begin to understand the power you are, the Presence in which you live.

Saint Augustine talked about folks who went out looking for Spirit. Nowadays people go to the Himalayas looking for God, or climb the Pyramids, thinking He's perched on top in the lotus position. (I've tried both. He wasn't.) Back in Saint Augustine's day, in about 350 AD, he said, "People travel to wonder at the heights of the mountains, at the huge waves of the sea, at the long courses of the river, at the vast compass of the ocean, at the circular motion of the stars and they pass by themselves without wonder."

Right where you are, God is. Realize your responsibility is to allow your consciousness to move to a state that realizes the Presence. Not a dualistic aspect of "me and God"—rather, "It is God expressing as me." This realization heals! it opens the doors. This realization will calm our reaction to any turbulence, and get us out of any predicament in which we find ourselves.

When we are able to be in the Presence, amazing transformations will take place in our lives. What is essential is for us to realize the presence of God, not outline it and tell God, "Okay, this is how you have to do it..." as if our impotent mind can outfigure the omniscient Presence. If you truly believe you can't outthink God, let God handle it. Let Spirit figure out how to take care of your world and your life. If you're dealing with some big turbulence in your life you don't have to tell God how to heal it. It is up to you to fly into the Presence. Get quiet and know God as yourself. When you know this, It naturally knows how to heal. It guides the universe and the galaxy. I promise you It can take care of your life. But so often we get involved in attempting to tell Spirit how to do it. I want you to know it is not by our might and it is not by our power that we heal situations—it's by consciousness! It's by the realization of the presence of God. When you realize the Presence, it puts your mind to rest. It's called Peace. When you realize the Presence, your mind quiets down. All anxiety quiets down. It's up to you to be able to go inside of yourself to the inner instruments, and let your mind be at rest in the midst of your storm. It's not about going to God for anything—for yourself or for anyone. God is all. It's given it all already. When you can come to this realization healing happens in the appropriate ways in your life—whether physical healing, emotional healing or situation healing. Maybe not in the way you thought it should be, but in ways that are appropriate. You have to be willing to go inside and look.

So often people are into denial and say, "Hey, this stuff doesn't exist. It's all an illusion. I heard it in my metaphysical teachings; all this manna, all this stuff out here is just an illusion." Well, you tell the IRS they're an illusion and see how far it gets you. Tell a doctor who says you've got something going on inside your body, or tell a relationship that's about ready to crack, "Oh, you're just an illusion. Our relationship doesn't really exist." How much good is it going to do you? It's not about denial of what is in this world! It's about looking at what is in this world and moving through the storm, and seeing the presence of God. It's coming to an understanding of Its relationship to you.

If you're using your energy to hold the circumstances away, you're fighting it. You are in a dualistic battle. The winds of turbulence will whip the steering wheel right from your hands and flip your plane upside down, spinning you out of control. It's time to go within and remove yourself from the fight—not by your effort, but by the realization of the presence of God, which will lift you to a stable atmosphere, flying with Spirit, unafraid to look at anything.

A Loose Cannon

In his novel, *Ninety-Three*, Victor Hugo told of a ship out in a raging storm. All of a sudden the crew heard this horrific clanging inside the hold and realized the cannon inside the ship had been knocked loose. Every time a wave smacked the ship to one side, the cannon would crash against the inside of the hold. Then it would get it the other way and crash against the other side. The crew knew if this continued the cannon would go right through the hull and the ship would go down, not because of the storm raging from the outside, but because what was inside had not been tied down properly. The story goes on about two brave guys who go down and tie up the cannon.

In our lives, when the storms are raging on the outside, it's a reflection of what is on the inside. It is time to go within, not patch it up on the outside, not take a pill or get a few extra grand to get out of debt. If you created debt, you are probably going to create another one unless you understand what was the cause from within. Isn't it amazing the way this works? If you have a challenge and you patch up the effect but don't deal with the cause (or cannon), the loose stuff inside, it's going to show up again. What is essential is to come to the realization of the presence of God in your life. What does this realization look like? I'll give you a hint: You are wonderful, a child of God, worthy of living life in a place of peace and rest, and capable of sailing the rough seas with assurance.

I hear stories time and time again of how amazing transformations are going on. It's not because a person is a healer and they bring power. It's because they are like a little child uttering the ABCs without knowing the first thing about prayer, but they are in the "heart-place," in true realization, they are into life's flight.

Where Are You Lined Up?

Whom do you serve? Some are serving sickness, others struggle. There are some serving their jobs. Still others serve their relationships, their checkbooks or their employers. Ask yourself, "Whom do I serve?" Where's your consciousness? Where are you lined up for takeoff? Are you worried and anxious over finances, over relationship, over body, over form? If so, you'll have a turbulent flight. Spirit is ever present, waiting to serve you. How do you want to align with this energy? Are you choosing to align with the fears, the worries, the concerns and the anxieties—the turbulence in your life? Remember: "It's done unto you as you believe."

When we can look fear right in the face, we can see our fear is just one piece of the puzzle. Being able to look at those pieces allows one to see some kind of pattern for good woven into them, fitting together and unfolding. This kind of living Faith will create a new you. It will lift you to a new and higher altitude of calm. We can look at conditions in our lives without being at the effect of them. When we have this kind of Faith, we will begin to experience the manifestations within our lives that our hearts desire—those desires coming from on High.

I sometimes remember Moses, who wandered through the desert for 40 years. Forty years is a long time to hold on to one's Faith—to believe in the vision and to know the truth. He had a lot of turbulence going on in those 40 years. There were people rebelling, melting down their gold and creating false idols. Yet he went to the mountaintop, gaining altitude and perspective by climbing above the turbulence. He came back shining because he'd seen the burning bush that could not be consumed. He had a Faith. He was able to take a look at turbulence that could stir up fear and confusion—people uniting against him—and he held the Faith. Holding the vision, he remained calm and his clarity was embraced.

When we find ourselves in a situation stirring turbulent, churning energy inside of us—the negativity—it is not time to get people to jump on our bandwagon. We can cite challenges to substantiate a position of fear and get people to rally with our turbulent vision. Rather, it's time now to know the Truth. Often people say, "I've got this one handled." But they don't really handle it; they just kind of change the face of the condition in their lives. It's like exchanging one devil for another in their world. I'm not talking about the guy with the pitchfork and the tail. I'm talking about the challenges—changing one face of a relationship to another face of a relationship, or one illness for another, or one financial crisis for a new one. The same kind of condition shows up within one's life once again. "Having it handled" is about changing consciousness. It is about changing one's inner experience. It's not about getting people to believe in the facts and the world of phenomenon. Rather, it's about going to the mountaintop and having the Faith—even if it takes 40 years. This is the way you fly from fear to Faith, from turbulence to peace, to the "air space" of knowing, of trusting and believing.

God has not given us the spirit of fear, but one of love. When you start practicing these principles, if it doesn't seem to happen right away in your world, remember to give it some time. Follow your inner instruments to that "air space" of faith, knowing "This too shall pass." You're greater than the storm that appears to surround you. You are a unique expression of the Divine, and right where you are, God is there to guide you through faith to the "air space" of perfect peace.

CHAPTER FIVE

FUELED BY LOVE

One story of Gandhi serves as a beautiful
example of a loving individual.
Getting on a train, he stumbled
as it was taking off and lost his shoe
on the track. As he jumped onto
the train and straightened up,
he then took off his other shoe
and threw it onto the track.
His wife asked him what he was doing
and he said, "Well, the poor soul who
finds only one shoe could use the other."

Before any and every flight, I never fail to take the time to contemplate and calculate how much fuel is necessary for my trip. Basic? Certainly, but every jet, rocket or small aircraft needs fuel in order to take off, as well as enough fuel to sustain its airborne status. While it may seem trivial compared to modern navigational devices and high-tech equipment, there's no denying fuel is vital to any sort of flight.

You're like a rocket on the launch pad, ready to take off and fly to the farthest reaches of your dreams. You may be intellectually equipped with knowledge of great esoteric truths and the metaphysical laws of faith, but if you've forgotten the fuel, true flight is impossible. Our fuel is love—and energy that is the presence of God right where you are. When you choose to feel the presence called love or a "connection with the Source," whose supply is infinite, you begin to realize you are Divine. You are the Spirit of God seeking expression as your life. With this realization you're able to step out and move into this love energy.

Have you ever been given the message (though perhaps in subtler words) that being in a space of love means giving your power away? Our culture often says, "Being in love is kind of silly. Being in love is a weak position." Have you ever received this kind of input? Yet, silly is going on a journey without fuel. (And aren't you traveling through life?) Some cultures have learned love is a very spiritual experience, and teach that coming from love we find a power, a strength and a knowingness. We find an assurance, because we begin to be more connected with who we are. There is clarity when we allow ourselves to come from Spirit.

One story of Gandhi serves as a beautiful example of a loving individual. Getting on a train, he stumbled as it was taking off and lost his shoe on the track. As he jumped onto the train and straightened up, he then took off his other shoe and threw it onto the track. His wife asked him what he was doing and he said, "Well, the poor soul who finds only one shoe could use the other." This was just the natural expression of love, not because he was thinking, but because he was coming from the heart. He was an individual who was able to step into eternity when the opening was there. He had the courage and conviction. He never thought of the fact that somebody might sit there and criticize, questioning what he was doing. Instead, there was an impulse inside of him that just fueled him into action.

Intimate with the Inexhaustible

If you allow this love energy to impel you to take action in all you do in your life, you will find yourself being excited about life. This excitement is as stimulating and rewarding as anything. When you solved a problem, how did you feel? When you wrote a poem, how did you feel? When you cooked a magnificent dinner for yourself or shared it with someone, how did you feel? Sharing a message on Sunday, I can't begin to put the loving wonder into words. This kind of energy, which is the love of life, is the fuel that I'm speaking about. It's not only available in those magical moments when you step into the flow; it's also available to encourage you to know the flow is always flowing. The choice of whether you buy into the fallacy of a fuel shortage or become intimate with the inexhaustible Source is yours. This Source is always there to reveal Itself in your life as passion, bliss and love.

A wonderful Bible verse tells us, "Those that love not, know not God, for God is love." This is pretty clear. If you want to know God, it's up to you to begin to know love—to begin to see the presence of God in all things. Calm your world down enough to get the lessons and decide you don't want to buy into those headlines or the world of phenomena. Desire to come from this Source, this fuel of Love that moves a person in the direction of fulfillment, or joy and success. Does the fuel gauge of the outside world, whose source is able to run out, measure your fuel or input, or does it come from an inexhaustible reservoir seeking to express through you? You have to clear your mind from the bombardment of the grand pictures creeping over you when you slip into those alpha states in front of the television. Your mind will need to be calmed after the talk around the water cooler at work, where violent thoughts about the day's headlines were en-tertained—tales of a bus highjack, terrorist threats or the next evil force that wants to nuke us.

Look at what we fill our minds with. We hear, read and discuss the headlines in court cases as opposed to contemplating God or doing our spiritual reading. Some would rather sit in front of the TV and watch news (because "you have to be aware of what's go-ing on"), instead of sitting down and meditating to connect with Source, fueling up and allowing the loving fuel to flow, thereby finding passion in life. Some people actually spend more time in the morning shaving, putting makeup on, getting dressed and fueling up on their coffee, than they spend contemplating God. Remember: The spiritual stuff is your true fuel.

How Do You Use the Fuel?

There's a story of a guy named Kenneth, who was in junior high. He got really excited when the Special Olympics were coming to his school. Kenneth was running in two races, and his mom and dad were there during the first race, cheering him on. He crossed the finish line first, and stood proudly as he was awarded his blue ribbon. The crowd cheered and he was filled with excitement, clutching his ribbon and loving the sound of applause. Then, when he was running the second race, he was out in front again and about to cross the finish line. Again the crowd was cheering—and he stopped. He stepped off the track.

Later, his mom lovingly pointed out that if he hadn't stopped running he would have won the race. Very innocently, Ken-neth replied, "But Mom, I already have a blue ribbon and Billy doesn't."

What a great attitude! When flying, you're asked, "How's your attitude?" This means, "Are you flying straight and level, or are you all messed up and all over the place due to the inconsistency of your flying?"

Kenneth's attitude was straight and level—a natural love, which means not being attached to the outside. It's being part of the flow, coming from a place of love. Touching the heart, this is "the power of increase." It's a power that inspires us to give from a spirit of love, shaking us free of any apathy we might find ourselves stuck in. It allows us to remember who we truly are, which is the presence of God. The presence of God is seeking expression in and through you, and as you. God is always being God. God is always being God revealing Itself through you. God is revealing Itself as you now!

This love, this presence of God I speak of, is all and constant and abiding. It isn't just available in times of triumph. It's there to express, to share and to flow during those times that appear the most adverse or challenging as well.

There was a baby by the name of Jason, who was born with a congenital heart defect that couldn't be corrected with anything other than a heart transplant. While Jason was waiting on a donor, his mom developed liver cancer, which had spread to the point that it was inoperable. From birth on, Jason lived his life on medication and was continuously at the doctor's office. At the age of five, he actually had to have a tube put into his chest to run into one of his main veins. He wore a pump in a backpack that gave him medicine directly. Yet this little guy would not let his experience deny him one moment of his life. He loved to run around, and sometimes he was even a little terror. Not only would he play with his backpack on, since he sometimes also had to have oxygen, he pulled it along in his little wagon behind him. His mom would joke with him that she would have to dress him in bright yellow so that when she looked out the window she could quickly find him out in the yard wherever he was darting around and playing. Jason would giggle at that one. Well, even this little guy, in his dynamic expression in life, was unable to combat the effects of his failing heart. His heart grew weaker as he took a turn for the worse. No donor had been found and it was obvious that he was going to die. His mom's health was also rapidly declining. She had a conversation with Jason, telling him about death, about his heart, and that she was going to be joining him in Heaven very shortly, so he shouldn't be worried or concerned. Little Jason proceeded to get worse.

Two days before he died, Jason was lying in his hospital bed and called over one of his friends. His voice a whisper, he told him, "I might be dying soon, but I'm not afraid. I'm going to go to Heaven and you know what? Make sure they dress me in bright yellow because my mom's going to meet me in Heaven soon. I'm going to be playing and I want her to be able to spot me real soon."

This little guy had a faith beyond one that can be taught. It was an understanding that could not be learned from the outside—a conviction and assurance that love gave him. Touching him in a deep way, it could not be taken away by adversity or challenge. This love and presence was constant, abiding—all and ever present. It's there for each of us.

Enough to Move Through the Ceiling

A certain amount of fuel is necessary to reach your destination. When airborne, there will be times when you run into crosswinds and need more fuel to see you through. It never hurts to have more fuel or love than you think you'll need. In order to fuel up, I encourage you to take some quality time with yourself. Recognize you are Spirit, your essence in love—pure-grade, top-quality fuel. As you begin to know more and more clearly what your source is, you will be willing to take a little bit greater risk in life. If you want to experience love, you have to love. Just as the law of cause and effect is true across the board, cause and effect is true with love. People tend to get their parameters set: "I can be this vulnerable. This is how much love I can handle." They set limits and decide, "That's about it." But as you begin to take time with yourself and touch the essence of your being, which is beyond words and limits, you come to recognize and realize, "Hey, it really is safe. It's Spirit out there. I can move right through the ceiling of clouds I envisioned. The person I'm looking at is really *God*." This is the higher vibration I was speaking about. Then you're willing to share more of your heart and your soul and your spirit without being concerned about whether or not you are going to be loved back, because the truth is that you are lovable. All of you—not part of you—all that you are is lovable.

Oscar Wilde said, "As you begin to love yourself, you will have started one of life's longest romances." Somewhere around ten—the age differs in some people's lives, but somewhere along the line—many are told it's not good to love yourself. When was the last time you looked in the mirror and asked yourself, "Hey, good lookin', how's it going?" When was the last time you looked at yourself and realized, "Hey, I'm Spirit." That's the truth of you. You're pure-grade, top-quality, super fuel. You've received your airworthiness certificate and you can fly! Coming to this awareness allows you to participate in life and relationships knowing, "What I have to offer is a tremendous deal, a tremendous package. I participate in the creation of the Divine expression here on Earth."

Sometimes people stray into a place of judgment or to a spot where they're missing or lacking and focus on what's not working in their lives. They go out to seek a relationship to fill the void. Loving a person in order to fill a void, they believe this person brings what is lacking in their world. They say, "I love this individual because they bring what I lack in my life." This is not the basis of a healthy relationship! You are a whole individual. When two whole individuals come together, they bring their uniqueness, their individuality and their diversity. Offer yourself to life as a whole person—not as a person looking for someone to bring you peace or to bail you out, or as someone looking for a partner to fill a space of lack.

People can get caught up in the world of effects. They put their faith in effects, as opposed to the power of God. God's presence moves from within one's soul, from within one's own being. Love is here. It comes from opening up to it. The more you open, the greater thrust you have. However, when you're looking on the outside you are missing the essence. I watch people selling themselves out trying to placate those potential threats, trying to quiet them down. They go around trying to be nice and calm so they can win approval, as though they were helpless children growing up, trying to win parental approval by being good. This is not where love comes from. It comes from inside you and then the outside begins to reflect it back. It's not something you can win. It's not something you can get from the outside. Haven't you tried to win approval enough times in life to have learned this lesson? Get these love lessons of life so you don't go repeating those patterns! Take heed of the flight advisories life gives you, so you may soar beyond the ceiling you've been attempting to reach.

Haven't you also discovered you can't make anybody get it? You cannot browbeat anybody into love: "You will love me!" We try to teach them, force them into getting how wonderful I am, or you are, or this is, or that teaching is. You cannot force anybody to Spirit. You can be an example and maybe they'll catch it; maybe they'll be inspired and enthused, and maybe they won't. This is no indication of who you are. Still, you cannot force anybody to love. It's time to surrender to Spirit. It's time to let go. It's time to believe the power of God *will* prevail. Begin to use the power and the energy you have to realize your own connection with God. Use your mind and your soul to work on this connection with your Source. Watch it take form in your life.

Flying near huge, towering thunderclouds can very quickly and dramatically teach a pilot about flying—if he survives nature's lesson. Or one can choose to learn gently. Sometimes this gentle approach doesn't bring the quick, dramatic and painful lessons or those immediate results of the drama received from the romantic tension. What tends to produce in form in your life is a reflection of the work and time you have taken. This love energy will begin to radiate from you like a beacon of light. Those who see and are attracted to this beacon of light will support and love you for who you are.

Too often, I watch people trying to "hook" one. Do you know what I mean? "Boy, I got a good catch this time. It's a keeper." Most people know how to dress up and smell good and use their bodies with the best of them to catch one. But if you end up having to use your energy to hold the person, it is *your* energy, not the Divine flow. Haven't you done this one enough? Hasn't life already taught you that's not the way? Be willing to step into the flow. Love tends to come back into your life. You'll come from a sense of wholeness because you will have done your work to connect with your Source. You will be fueled from the Divine with that movement that we call love. The awareness is love energy.

This revelation, jubilation and excitement is the movement of Spirit.

When you are expressing from this kind of place, you're not out there looking for an intimate relationship; you are being intimate with life—a lover in life. This energy comes back to you in love reflected in a smile, the twinkle of an eye, the right connections out in your business world, or an unfoldment of a challenge within a family or any other relationship. Spirit knows whatever is appropriate in your life. You don't need to tell God, "Hey, I need you to fill this hole, this lack, this space." Spirit knows. It's done a pretty good job of guiding things up to this point. What is essential is for you to know Spirit. What is essential is for you to love yourself enough to fill the fuel tank and begin to discover the presence of God that you are, and to surrender to the presence and the process. By surrender, I'm not saying you surrender to another person. Rather, you surrender to the presence of God—to the love energy that is. Surrender to the power, to Divine essence, to the energy that moves. Such surrendering is nothing you can really plan on. You can think you are willing to do this, but you'll never really know until you spontaneously let go in the moment.

Get out there and give God a moving target to hit. As we fully commit ourselves to Spirit, to the Divine, what we will start seeing when we look into another person's eyes is God. And as they look back into your eyes, they will also be seeing God. You'll find the relationships you are in are beautiful. You will be loving from the bottom of your soul, from the depth of your being and from the breadth of your heart. You will find the people in your life are so blessed because they are getting this love from you. You will also find your life blessed because the same kind of love will be coming back from them. Fuel up on the love lessons life has been giving you.

How Much Can You Handle?

The greatest commandment is, "Love the Lord your God with your whole heart, your whole soul and your whole mind." The second one is, "Love your neighbor as yourself." You may think of your neighbor as the person sitting next to you, or the person living next door, but metaphysically speaking, apart from literal interpretations, your neighbor can be any of those things that come into your life and mind. Think about this. It includes any of those thoughts moving into your consciousness. Those are also your neighbors—whether it's a person, a place, a thing or a thought in your field of awareness. If you could learn to love these as you love yourself, as much as you love God, you will find you're no longer in a place of disparity, holding on to anger, animosity, resentment, hatred or bitterness. You will bring yourself back into a place of oneness with God, and move beyond any type of fear into a place of rapture, into a place of ecstasy. You will be propelled to a place of ecstatic joy and happiness in your life. This stratosphere allows you to be moving in a place of bliss, of such connection and knowingness. Your countenance will shine from this high place of rapture, as you know you have been with God and are an expression of the Divine.

Remember when you first got involved in an intimate relationship? Right at the very beginning, one of the things you brought to the relationship was some quality time. Do you remember this? When was the last time you brought this kind of quality time to yourself? When was the last time you took yourself out on a date and were with yourself and your being, and just sat there and contemplated a tree growing, or a tomato "tomatoing," and looked inside yourself and your being? This is refueling, because this is where you begin to experience love. This is where you begin to touch the Spirit that is real, that is personal, which *you* know. As we talk about love, we talk about the joy and the elation and all those wonderful things, but they're words. I'm attempting to articulate and touch something ineffable. It cannot really be verbally or literally communicated.

Have you ever just sat there and watched a little baby giggle and laugh? Weren't you absolutely caught up in the rapture of the moment? You were so involved with the little child that words could not describe to somebody in the next room what you were going through. But you were absolutely part of it. Well, love is like this. It is so wonderful that you cannot begin to put it into words. So I want to ask you, how much love can you handle? That's one of the questions you can continue to ask yourself: "How much love can I handle?" Because the truth is: God is all and God is love—or this Life Force is all—so there is as much as you can handle in your life. Are you ready to enlarge your fuel tank?

If you are staying in your head, attempting to describe what love is, you're missing out. It's time for you to take some quality time with yourself and discover the quality of *your* being. How much love can you handle? Let me assure you, there is even more than that available to you.

American existential psychologist Rollo May said, "The amazing thing about love is that it is the best way to get to know yourself." One of the best things you can offer a relationship is your spiritual potential. You come into the relationship whole, but life is about flow. Life is about unfoldment. Life is about evolution. Life is about growth. You do not know what next week, next month, next year is going to contain. If you are willing to bring your honesty and your truth, your vulnerability and a willingness to share your spiritual potential within the relationship, then you have a magnificent foundation to build upon. It may grow together, or it may grow apart, but apart does not need to be bad. It could be wonderful.

I can understand love at first sight; this makes sense. Loving someone as years go on can be more difficult. It takes a little bit of work, a little bit of time. But when you're willing to bring your spiritual potential, things begin to happen. You need to take the time to love! This is the price of a full heart—taking the time to love. It's the price of experiencing a life filled with passion and excitement and unlimited possibilities unfolding. Remember to take the time. It's what it takes to experience an increase of love in your life.

Where there is love, great love, miracles happen. Magic appears within a relationship, healing happens in the body and affairs. Where there is love you become rejuvenated, revitalized. You come up with new idea and new angles to your business, and you are willing to step out in ever-greater ways.

How much love are you willing to handle? Are you willing to take the time to be with yourself and recognize the top-grade fuel you are? Setting aside this time allows you to realize the essence of your being. This essence is Spirit—love that is pure, wonderful and Divine. This Love has the answer, whatever the question. Yet coming to this awareness does take time. We exhaust ourselves by spending so much of our lives getting—getting the relationship, getting the place, getting the job, getting the reward. We have put ourselves in a recession, to the point where we are paying back now what we spent yesterday.

So remember to take the time. That's the cost of experiencing a life filled with joy, love, happiness and well-being.

In your life, when you know Spirit is there, when you know the essence of your being is love, you are willing to take a little greater step. When you know the truth of who you are, you are willing to take a little greater risk in loving, in your vulnerability. How much love can you handle? It depends upon how much risk you are willing to take in your life. It's about having the relationship with yourself to know what's in there, going beyond those experiences you have labeled unlovable. You've got to go beyond that point if you want to grow and expand in your world.

When fueled by love, one is willing to be vulnerable, willing to take the time and the risk to fly through the ceiling to eternity, to reach out one's hand. In that moment Spirit speaks magical words, touching the heart and allowing one to remember. I encourage you to remember the truth of the top-grade, super-quality fuel of love and the presence of God that you are—remembering your flight's very source and energy fills you right here and now.

CHAPTER SIX

IN-FLIGHT SERVICE

When we're coming from the heart,

we are listening to Spirit,

we are being divinely moved.

We are no longer being motivated

from the exterior,

but rather from the interior

of our own being,

where the true spiritual gauges lie.

We are being motivated from a place

of absolute connectedness with Spirit.

As the pilot of your life, you are in command, responsible for everything in your world. This responsibility includes being of service where Spirit moves you to act, to express and to give. Such service can even mean sitting in as copilot, supporting someone who's maneuvering through storms on their flight through life.

Ernest Holmes wrote:

It's easy enough to rush around shouting that there are no sick people, but this will never heal those who appear to be sick. It's easy to proclaim that there are no needy. Anyone can say this, whether he be wise or otherwise. If we are to prove such state-

ments to be facts in our experience, we shall be compelled to do
more than announce a principle, no matter how true it may be.

We must be compelled to do more than just announce a principle. Beyond simply espousing the truth of a principle, using it requires becoming more assertive in our lives. It's not a passive philosophy. You have to do more than plot your course, even if it's perfect and true. You have to take off, fly and navigate through all that comes your way.

Saint Francis of Assisi said, "The deeds you do may be the only sermon some people will hear today." Your actions are like the flow of Spirit coming through you. I realize sometimes in our lives we don't feel very spiritual. I realize sometimes in our lives the God essence just seems to be blocked. During those times, if we allow that Essence to transmit our course to our hearts by faith, we'll find ourselves acting on our willingness to allow Spirit to flow through us. Are you serving Spirit by living in Truth?

Tory Matthews moved from Southern California to Arizona, where she got a job with the animal shelter. One day Tory got a call that a young boy's iguana had gotten scared and run up a tree, then fallen out of the tree into the swimming pool. She ran over to the house with a big net and scooped the iguana out of the swimming pool, but the iguana was lifeless, as it had been lying in the pool for some time. She looked at the little boy, who was extremely sad, and then she looked at this hideous-looking thing. In her head she debated, "You can do CPR for people, you can do CPR for dogs...no, this thing is a little too ugly." Yet, she saw the little boy's caring and she just couldn't tell him his iguana had died, so she went ahead and gave CPR to the iguana and it came back to life. She revived this ugly reptile (well, probably not ugly to another iguana). This was a result of the little boy having enough faith in a savior, faith in some kind of outside person showing up. Looking at this little boy and seeing the love he had for his pet, she couldn't say no to what appeared ugly. In our lives, there may be times we look at people who appear ugly or situations that look hideous and horrendous. If we can just remember the love of the Father, the love of the Presence—of God—is still right there in the very midst, we will them be able to step through the appearance, the form, the effect in our world. But we've got to have faith.

There's an African proverb that says, "When deeds speak, words are nothing." What are your deeds speaking? Are your deeds showing you have the courage in your life to create, to heal rifts of separation, to serve? Are your deeds showing you are stepping into the Flow? If they are, your world is growing and expanding dramatically. If they are, you are sailing through the skies of life and able to assist others to soar also.

The heart knows what feels right. Not long ago, Seaside Church moved to a new location. The decision to do so was tough, and there was a lot of controversy concerning our move. As pilot-in-command, I had to stand strong in the vision and not succumb to the fears and doubts of others. My heart knew what felt right.

Recently, I had the opportunity to be out on the streets shaking some hands during a local street fair, where we had a booth right out in front of the church. It was wonderful to meet people I had never met and to see people I hadn't seen in a long time. The latter said they used to go down to our old place in Del Mar, but hadn't made their way to our new site. "Where are you now?" they'd ask. I was able to answer, "Right there," and point out our new location. It really felt good inside my heart to see how many lives we had touched by creating this space of love—a place without judgment, which supports individuals on their personal paths. It felt good to have people walk by, not recognize them, yet have them come up and say, "Seaside, yeah, that spiritual community touched me in a wonderful way."

The same day there were baskets for children at an orphanage we support in Tecate spread out all over our Sanctuary. There was a whole crew of people filling them with stuffed animals and food and toys. In the back room, someone was spray-painting the walls. The teens had a workshop going on in yet another room. Seeing all these different activities, my heart just knew we were doing something right where we were. It was really exciting to watch the vision of this center, this place of love and activity, being utilized. I was touched—it just felt so good! The heart knows of the joy of giving, of service. Through the heart, ways to serve can appear at every level of life.

Adding Your Touch

Currently one of the big things in the business seminar circuit is teaching people how to bring the personal touch to whatever position they are in. Some people just know this at heart level, having no need for a seminar to teach them. Carmen Parada is one of these people. Plump, with trails of laugh lines a predominant part of the map of wrinkles on her olive-colored face, Carmen is over 80 years of age, yet her daily acts of service still flow. She's the sort of person people are drawn to. Her presence and sincere interest inspire a sense of comfort. Every day, Carmen opens up her small booth along with the other vendors on a Southern California boardwalk. She then goes to work selling novelties and the pastries she bakes herself each day, being of service by sharing who she is with love. "What a beautiful baby," she beams at a young mother, pushing a stroller. Turning to dig into her box of "prizes," Carmen pulls out a colorful rattle and stoops to hand it to the delighted infant. "But lots of hugs and kisses from her mother will give her so much more happiness than any toy!" she reminds the mother with a smile. When a group of two or three young children stops to look over her wares, she reaches for her pastries and hands them each one. "Take these," she says, doling them out as she adds, "and remember to do what your mama tells you."

Where prizes and pastries are less appropriate, Carmen imparts kind words and Old World wisdom, first said in Spanish, then repeated in English: "A fair man is worth two," she exhorts a local judge. "Speaking and eating fish, you must be careful when doing both," she tells a woman who confides she's been very tempted to divulge some gossip she just heard about one of her co-workers. When the younger woman looks unconvinced, Carmen adds, "They say, 'If your mouth is closed no flies fly in.'" No judgment in her tone, she speaks with a gentle smile and a kind of "think-this-one-over-if-you'd-like" inflection. Often it's simply her smile and genuine caring, which shines from her dark eyes, that attract many of her regular customers. But they all agree that her words of wisdom also add charm to their day, although they also admit some of those proverbs need to be mulled over, and others must lose something in the translation: "A lazy person works twice as hard...One nail hits another nail out...It is just as big a sin to kill a cow as it is to hold one down...A dog that is barking can't bite...If you are among wolves you learn how to howl...Water that is not used to drink, let it run." Carmen has a graciously expressed adage for every occasion and conversation.

One lady confesses, "I used to come down to the boardwalk maybe once a week, but now I come every morning on my way to work to get my words of wisdom and pastry for the day."

Imagine what this does for the bottom line of Carmen's small business. Her attitude was one of kindness and faith. She wasn't saying, "Okay, I'm going to try to do good." Carmen was feeling good. It was connectedness. That harmonious expression allowed her life to continue to flow through her body—not just a miserable "Here I am at my age still going out to work every day and I'm just doing it to make money." She found the love and the passion in her work, and it was contagious. All of a sudden, at the flower vendor's booth, when the flowers would break off, instead of throwing them away the vendor would give them to the older ladies or the little girls browsing on the boardwalk, helping to pin them on. There was a guy selling incense and oil fragrances, who loved Mickey Mouse. He went out and bought thousands of Mickey Mouse stickers and pressed one on every bag he handed to a customer. That boardwalk became a hot spot to locals and tourists alike because these individual chose to connect, chose to feel—to express themselves.

So often in our lives we turn ourselves off, giving away our position as pilot-in-command. We say things like, "Well, I've got to act a certain way...to be a certain way within this relationship to win approval or love...act a certain way at work—you know it's the corporate way to present myself in a certain light." Doing this, little by little you begin to shut off and cap the authentic, unique, Divine, powerful expression that is seeking to move through you in ever-greater ways. As long as we are turning that off, it gets tougher and tougher to hear it, to see what it feels like. This is why I greatly encourage you to meditate, to take time to sit quietly, to be with yourself, so you will know not only what the power feels like, but also what your personal forecast is. It's not about what *I* say this power is. It's not about words. It's not about principles, and it's not about concepts. It's about knowing.

It's been said, "When you have entirely surrendered, everything you do will be a meditation." When we take the time to meditate, to know our own personal forecast, we move to a place of surrender to Spirit, where we are able to give, living our lives from a sense of absolute connection.

Prayer is really beyond words. In the classes we teach a great structure we call scientific prayer. We have definite techniques for praying, but it's not the words or the technique that's important. It is the essence—the feeling. As Victor Hugo said, "Certain thoughts are prayers. There are moments when, whatever be the attitude of the body, the soul is on its knees." Again, this comes with an open sense of connection to Spirit. When we give and serve from such a place, as expressions of the Divine flow, we know heights of joy and satisfaction that can never be taken from us.

A very successful Argentinean golf pro won a tournament and was given a wonderful check. Then came all the cameras, the hoopla and the hype that goes with winning a tournament—the joy in the clubhouse. When it all died down at the end of the day and the parties were over, he was walking back to his car all alone when a woman came out and congratulated him, praising him for the wonderful tournament he had just won. She went on to share that her young son was gravely ill and would probably die, confiding she had no money to pay for the doctor bills. So the golf pro took his winning check, signed it over and pressed it in her hand, saying, "Make some good days for your young child."

It's a beautiful story. A week later, the golf pro was sitting in the clubhouse talking with some friends when one of the officials from the Gold Association came up to him and said, "Hey, we heard what you did. One of the caddies out there saw you give that lady your check. Well, we want you to know the lady's a fraud. She's not married. Her son's not dying. As a matter of fact, she doesn't even have a child. You've been taken."

"You mean there isn't a sick little boy?" the golf pro asked.

"No," the official answered.

"That's the greatest news I've heard all week!" the golf pro cheered.

Flying With Heart

When you are landing through the haze and fog, and at the last minute you finally see the runway before you touch down, it's a great feeling—a relief. All the challenges up to that point no longer matter.

Giving from the heart, from a place of caring and love, not because you're looking to get back, but because you are living from a place of connection, takes one out of getting caught up in doing good—being a "do-gooder" by trying to do the "right thing."

Coming from the heart means acting with compassion—feeling with a fellow human being, sharing their pain or their joy. It doesn't mean feeling right or feeling "better than." Compassion is a strength awakened by an awareness of a common humanity. Creating those connections our hearts crave and require, it embraces an acceptance of the fact that in our deepest being, at times we all feel powerless and would welcome love and understanding.

Compassion comes from a place of love, from knowledge of our likeness as human beings. It helps heal our rifts or disconnection. From this place of love and giving, compassion is a seed of strength with all its roots and blossoms spiritual.

Genuine compassion with its inherent empathy isn't always born of having experienced similar circumstances in life. Sometimes it's simply recognition of someone else's feelings of pain and a genuine desire to support them in their healing. This can be service in its purest form. Sometimes it's received from unlikely sources.

Betty had lost her husband of 44 years to cancer, which took his life only two months after it was diagnosed. Having gone through six months of grieving, feeling as if she was finally at the other side of her pain and had reached a point of acceptance, she went shopping one Saturday. Standing in the aisle of a large department store, Betty picked up a silk scarf, fingering its feathery texture and studying its patterns; then she glanced at her watch. Seeing it was two o'clock, she thought, "Oh, I'd better get going. Leo will be getting home from playing cards soon." Her husband, Leo, had played bridge every Saturday afternoon, and come home at the same time following his game. Suddenly, realizing her husband wouldn't ever be home again and she had actually forgotten it for that space of time, Betty broke down in tears in the aisle of the department store.

A young man of about 20, who happened to be shopping there as well, saw her sobbing and approached her. Placing his arm around her shoulder, he asked gently, "Oh, what is it? What's wrong?"

In her grief, Betty spilled out her story with her tears as he stood there listening and allowing her to weep on his shoulder. Here was a man more than 40 years younger than she, raised in a totally different era, a complete stranger, yet his genuine compassion—his understanding of pain and his desire to be kind and to help alleviate it—touched her and helped heal that moment of pain.

When we're coming from the heart, we are listening to Spirit; we are being divinely moved. We are no longer being motivated from the exterior, but rather from the interior of our own being, where the true spiritual gauges lie. We are being motivated from a place of absolute connectedness with Spirit. When we do so, we're not caught up in trying to appear a certain way. We will be in absolute integrity with who we are. This integrity comes when we are able to shift our reliance from the external to the internal. In so doing, we are going to watch our flight through life be one that is absolutely exquisite. As long as we are out there trying to do the right thing, it's going to be empty, shallow and hollow. Your transmitter is revealing your course and people who are truly watching are not fooled; they know where you are.

Bengali yogi and guru Paramahansa Yogananda said, "Etiquette without sincerity is like a beautiful but dead woman." Etiquette without sincerity—doing it without the heart, just acting because one is supposed to act—is not what we're about. We're about being motivated from the heart. As long as we are alienated from our true Self, the right choices are going to be hard to make. If we are not connected with our Higher Being we don't know what our inner self sounds like and the "radio transmission" makes no sense because it sounds garbled.

Hearing the Control Tower

We all have a place inside us, a direct communication with the control tower, a deep connection with Source that we're able to hear and feel. When we're in tune with this consciousness it shines. We're able to have the faith, conviction and love to be a minister of that Light. People often ask, "Where is your Church?" Well, for this person on Monday morning it's in the courthouse; for that person over there it's in the medical building; for this person over here it's in the home; and for that person it's out there on the street, just sharing their ministry wherever they are. Being of service is not about one person in one place. It's about each of us going into the world, knowing and keeping the faith of the magnificence of our being in the midst of whatever challenges there might be, and knowing that keeping the faith brings the Light into times of darkness. You are Spirit expressing—magnificent. When keeping the faith, your life will reflect this. Should you encounter doubt, contact the control tower, which has an elevated perspective of the larger picture. It is a free service always there to support you in finding your way back on course.

If you want to move beyond the struggle, scarcity and lack, it is essential to step into the flow. You do this by getting involved with the givingness of life. Not long ago, we saw something phenomenal happen in our nation—the President called a Summit on volunteerism. Former Presidents Ford, Bush and Carter were there, as well as Nancy Reagan on behalf of her husband. Carter was saying now is the time if you are willing to get involved. It's no longer about the government doing it. We don't need another policy. We don't need another welfare handout. What's essential is for one-on-one connections to take place. What Carter challenged us to do was to step beyond where we are comfortable in our lives and go into the inner city. It's easy to talk prosperity here in North San Diego County, and I enjoy doing prosperity seminars in Beverly Hills; those are good spots. But what Carter was challenging us to do was to go into a city where all they know is fear.

Colin Powell said, "If you could just give 30 minutes a week, it would make a difference."

President Clinton said, "If we serve each other and if we work with each other, we will make sure that our diversity is a rich resource to make our union more perfect—not an instrument for national undoing." This isn't saying we give up who we are. We don't have to give up our authentic self. It's saying we should share who we are. You are the pilot-in-command, and the filing of your unique flight plan adds to the rich diversity. This includes being proud to share your talents through service, with whomever is moving in your direction.

Oprah Winfrey pointed out that this is a very exciting time because we are now able to set up mentoring programs for children and safe places for them to go after school. This is givingness. This type of giving will take one out of the place of "want" and into the flow. When you are giving, you're not into a place of survival; you are in a place of "flow"—a place where Spirit expresses through you.

What Are You Thinking?

What is your predominant thought during your flight's course on a daily basis? If you want to know, take a look at what's materializing in your life. American essayist Ralph Waldo Emerson said, "You are what you think about, all day long." The Bible says, "As a man thinks, so he is." So what is your predominant though as you fly through the skies of life? Are you thinking of the reasons why you can't get involved? "It's a good plan they put out there, but I can't get involved because of...(this or that)." Or is your predominant thought, "How can I find 30 minutes?" I encourage people to organize ways where others can get more involved in service. It's great because there are always passengers who want to be traveling in a common direction for good. Take a look at your predominant thought when some ideas come forward. Do you get excited about them or do you come up with a reason why they can't be done? Do you say, "Woe is me! I finally have my world held together just right, if nobody shakes it too much. If nobody rocks the boat, I'm going to be able to make it through this timeline called life." Life is about growth. It's about excitement. It's about activity.

Just look at the power there. If you want to experience increase, you have to open up and give. Listening to stories of service, I hear of people coming forward who never have done so before, and I watch as these people break free through community outreaches and other types of service. What has happened in the consciousness of some is the occurrence of something much like drugged apathy. They are just doing what it takes—the brain-numb experience in life, which allows them to deal with their days, going through the routines. You talk about cutting off the flow. Whack! Gone! But I truly believe people have inside of them that which is good—because It's God. I watch experiences like volunteer service awaken an individual's aliveness, his goodness, his passion, his desire to *be* in life. People miss out on so much in life because of numbness and apathy. Actually, the truth is we miss out on so much in life because we forget to ask for it. WE FORGET TO ASK. God is unlimited and yet we are the ones who put limits on our God. We're the ones who have juggled around in the world trying to rearrange ourselves so we can receive the good from Spirit. It's like trying to take the wheel away from the pilot, as opposed to stepping into the flow and being guided by our willingness to step out in a great way. You'll recognize the pilot is God, and you are on a Divine course.

Sometimes stepping out in a great way can mean service in little ways in our daily lives. In 550 BCE, the Greek slave Aesop said, "No act of kindness, no matter how small, is ever wasted." I'm reminded of one of the tales of the Holy Grail:

Once there was a boy who had to spend the night alone in

the forest to prove he had enough courage to become king. That night, while he sat next to the campfire alone in the forest, there appeared to him out of the fire a sacred vision. It spoke to him, saying, "Behold, I am the Holy Grail with power to heal the hearts of men." The boy was blinded by visions of power and greatness, and he reached into the flames to take the Grail, and was terribly burned. With time the King's wound grew and grew, and he spent all the wealth of his kingdom seeking to find the Holy Grail once again; in his quest he knew no peace, and he lost the ability to love and feel loved. Finally he lay in the bed of his deserted castle, sick and dying and all alone, when a jester happened upon the empty castle. Finding the king there alone, and not knowing who he was, the jester asked him, "What can I do for you, kind sir?"

The King replied, "I'm thirsty. Please give me some water." Taking the chalice from the table at the side of the bed, the jester poured some water and handed it to the King. As the King drank from the cup, there in his hands was the Holy Grail. He asked the jester in wonder, "How is it that you have found and brought to me that which my greatest and bravest and wisest could not?"

Shaking his head, the jester shrugged and answered, "I don't know—I just know you were thirsty so I gave you a drink."

Coming from a place of love, compassion and the sincere desire to give in service, a jester is able to present a King with the Holy Grail! The power to present the Grail lives in each of us.

I want to share with you a poem from an unknown author:

It's Up to You

> *One song can spark a moment.*
> *One flower can wake the dream.*
> *One tree can start a forest,*

And one bird can herald the spring.
One smile begins a friendship.
One handclasp lifts a soul.
One star can guide a ship at sea,
And one word can frame the gold.
One vote can change a nation.
One sunbeam lights a room.
One candle lights the darkness,
And one wrath can conquer gloom.
One step must start each journey.
One word must start each prayer.
One hope can raise our spirits,
And one touch can show we care.
One voice can speak with wisdom.
One heart can know what's true.
One life can make the difference.
You see—it's up to you.

You are that one life. You are the pilot-in-command of your flight through life, and you can be the copilot ready to assist another of God's pilots in flight. You'll find that as you begin to make a difference in your world, you begin to experience the joy of living.

CHAPTER SEVEN

III

TRUST THE FLOW

Allow yourself to be touched by Spirit,
so what occupies your mind
is the Spiritual Entity of your wholeness,
of your completeness.
Then when there is any area of your life
that can use some empowerment,
some healing, some flow, you will move
into a spiritual place and connect
with Spirit and allow your mind to be
filled with this Spiritual Entity.
So the words you speak don't come from
your human mind or the human
conditions that are prompting
your human mind, but instead,
you allow the thoughts,
the feeling to be moved
and prompted from within.

Taking off on a ski trip, I was heading up to British Co-lumbia on an airline that goes through Reno. There had been a lot of storms, and it just so happened Reno was under water that day—particularly the airport. I got to the San

Diego airport at about 9:00 on Thursday morning. I'd tried to call them the night before, but their lines had been busy for the preceding 24 hours. I hadn't realized the corporate offices were also under water.

I showed up at the airport and said, "I'm ready to go," to which they replied, "The flight has been canceled, but we can rebook you for Monday."

"No, I'm supposed to go skiing," I said. "My ride from Vancouver to Whistler will be waiting for me." They couldn't do it, they said. I told them they had to be able to do it. They insisted they couldn't do it.

There was someone who had been working on the counter people for over an hour before I got there, so I joined parties with them. All of a sudden a lot of other people were coming up and being turned away, but for some reason, they were attempting to reroute the four of us. Their airline wasn't flying, so they were trying to put us on another flight up to Los Angeles, but we missed that flight because they had been working so long to accommodate us. In the meantime, I heard there was a flight in Oregon on another airline, which could get us from Oregon on another airline, which could get us from Oregon to Vancouver at around midnight. "What about that one?" I asked. "It would work fine." They said, "Well, we don't have a reciprocal relationship with them." Right about this same time, they received a fax from the president of the airline saying, "No rerouting anybody." In the meantime, I was coaxing, "Come on, God. Come on, God. At this point, any airline will be just fine." I pleaded, "Why don't you just call someone and tell them to do this?" This creative rerouting and prayer went on for more than two-and-a-half hours.

Finally they were able to reroute us on a puddle-jumper from San Diego to Los Angeles, change airlines in Los Angeles to Oregon, and then there was a five-hour layover for this midnight flight I'd been praying for, which I knew was the answer to my prayer. All of a sudden, we arrived just in time to have a kind angel at the ticket counter put us on a Canadian subsidiary of the same strange airline we were flying on, which was going on strike the next day. It turned out to be a long day, but we got there.

Sometimes when we get attached to having it look a certain way (such as having my paid flight deliver what they promised, or my having to get there at a certain time), in a sense we begin to be in bondage. We get caught up in our expectations, as opposed to opening up to God and what is. Ernest Holmes wrote, "The Divine Plan is one of Freedom; bondage is not God-ordained. Freedom is the birthright of every living soul. All instinctively feel this. The truth points to freedom under Law. This, the inherent nature of man, is forever seeking to express itself in terms of freedom."

Our nature is forever seeking to express itself in terms of freedom, but as long as we get attached to expectations, thinking we are supposed to be praying in a certain way, then asking (or telling) God the way it's supposed to be, we are usurping God's power. Do you realize this? We are dealing with this Omniscience, which means It knows all, and we're trying to tell God what airline is the way to go?

If we just begin to enter into a higher state of awareness by stepping into the Presence and absolutely trusting it with all our heart and soul, choosing to know God in the midst, we will be freeing ourselves. Spirit knew I needed to get to Canada—knew all the airlines, is master of the control tower and knows all flight plans and how to get me there. I didn't, but from my limited perspective I tried telling God, "This is the way to do it."

This is a drastic change from many of the New Thought centers, which tell you to pray for the thing, visualize the specifics and create a mock-up of your desires—the Lotto, the relationship, the spouse. Traditional churches don't even pray for specifics; they ask, they beseech or beg. What we do in Religious Science is go to Spirit. We open our mind and consciousness and our soul to the very Source—the Thing Itself. This begins to lift us above and beyond our present level of circumstances within our lives. This is what It naturally does, because our focus begins to be at a higher place than the ticket counter, than the confusion, than the discord we find ourselves in. If we begin to put our mind and our awareness on the Presence, we will find a shift takes place: "I, of myself, can do nothing; it is the Father within."

How Deep Does Your Faith Go?

In December of 1914, Thomas Edison's laboratory burned to the ground. At the time it was worth over two million dollars, and it was a time when two million meant something. He had the lab insured for only a couple of hundred thousand dollars because he had it out of cement and was sure it was fireproof. But it burned to the ground, nonetheless. In the frenzy surrounding the fire his son, 24-year-old Charles, came looking for his dad. He found him standing very calmly outside, with the glow of the fire on his face and the wind blowing his white, distinguished hair. His heart just ached for his dad, who was 67 years old at this point, and all his life's work going up in flames. When he saw his son, the elder Edison said, "Hey, Charles, where is your mother?" Charles said, "I don't know." Thomas said, "Go get her; she'll never see anything like this again in her life." They stood there and just watched it.

The next day as he was going through the rubble, Thomas

Edison said, "You know there is a lot of value in disasters. All my mistakes have been destroyed. We can start anew." It was only three weeks later that he delivered the first phonograph to the world.

115

He kept the Faith. Trusting the flow, he didn't buy into earthly ways, the collective challenges, yet the headlines spoke of his ruin.

Ernest Holmes wrote:

> *Pure Faith is a spiritual conviction.* [See, it's not thinking, it is a spiritual conviction. It is an unshakable conviction.] *It is the acquiescence of the mind, the embodiment of an idea, the acceptance of a concept. If we believe that the Spirit, incarnated in us, can demonstrate, shall we be disturbed at what appears to contradict this? We shall often need to know that the Truth, which we announce, is superior to the condition we are to change. In other words, if we are speaking from the standpoint of the Spirit, then there can be no opposition to it!*

When we are speaking from the standpoint of Spirit, there can be no opposites.

I remember one summer watching a little guy, about three years old, in the shallow end of a swimming pool, holding onto his dad's neck. This little guy was just holding onto Dad, just so completely cool. He had it all under control. Then his dad started to walk down into the deep end a little bit at a time, saying pleasantly and playfully, "Deeper. Deeper. Deeper." You could see the panic come across this little guy's eyes. Now, Dad was still touching the bottom. There wasn't any problem, but there was fear in the little one's eyes. If he'd been big enough to step back and analyze the situation, he would have realized he couldn't touch the bottom any more in the shallow end than he could in the deeper end. He was as dependent upon his dad in the shallow end, when he was holding onto him, as he was when his dad walked into the deeper water. But all of a sudden the concept—a shift, the stuff—went on inside of him and began to create intensity within his life. In that moment, he was forming the unformed power in a way that created fear and anxiety in him.

We use the principle—we call forth this life essence in our lives with our fears, our worries, our anxieties and our concerns. God says, "Sure, you want to worry about it—let me give you something to worry about." You say, "How could it get worse?" God says, "Ah, let me show you how!" Get rid of that concept; remove it from your vocabulary. People say, "Why not me?" Well, Spirit will show you why not. Some challenge goes on in your world and you say, "Why me?" Well, Spirit will show you.

Form Houses Consciousness

Let's begin to get out of "why me" or "couldn't be worse" syndrome and begin to move to a greater place of understanding. So often we go to God looking for that Spiritual presence. We go to the Infinite Potential with our human condition, trying to come up with a human solution, which is absolutely a futile way to do it. If we are going to go to God, the Spiritual Energy, the Life Force, then let's go to It, open up to the answers and dump our attachment to the way we think it should turn out. Surrendering our position, say, "Okay, God, I'm choosing to use this Power by turning it over to a higher perspective that is for good." Then you become moved by It. Then you begin to take the necessary steps in your life to facilitate a vehicle, or an avenue, or a channel through which the form begins to materialize in your life.

The form houses your consciousness. Allow yourself to be moved by Spirit.

When someone goes to a medical doctor he gets a physical treatment. When someone works with a spiritual practitioner, he gets a spiritual treatment in the realm of mind, so we call it a spiritual mind treatment. It's a type of prayer or treatment. Ernest Holmes talked about treatment:

> *Treatment is an intelligent energy in the invisible world. It is a spiritual entity in the mental world and is equipped with power and volition—as much power and volition and there is faith in it given to it by the mind of the one using it—and, operating through the Law* [which is basically saying it is done at the level at which you believe], *It knows exactly how to work and what methods to use and just how to use them. We do not put the power into this word, but we do let the power of the Law flow through it and the one who most completely believes in this power will produce the best results.*

Allow yourself to be touched by Spirit, so what occupies your mind is the Spiritual Entity of your wholeness, of your completeness. Then when there is any area of your life that can use some empowerment, some healing, some flow, you will move into a spiritual place and connect with Spirit and allow your mind to be filled with this Spiritual Entity. The words you speak don't come from your human mind or the human conditions that are prompting your human mind, but instead you allow the thoughts and the feelings to be moved and prompted from within. Allow this to come through your mind and your awareness. Do you get the difference here?

It is that simple. We don't need to have these complex ways

of manipulating the Law; just step into the place that will lift us above and beyond to a state of higher awareness. It is there and It is this simple. Why do we want to complicate it? Sometimes it's difficult to grasp. Sometimes the world outside just doesn't get It. You want your friends and your family to get It, but they don't seem to be sufficiently receptive to the simplicity of the loving expression of life. As much as we want them to understand, if they aren't ready they won't hear It. It doesn't mean you can't live in a loving way, in an effortless flow of life, in the grace of God. You still can live It. You still can prove It. You can still be an expression, and you'll fly into the spiritual kingdom on Earth and some of your friends will come to you and say, "Hey, what is It? What are you doing?"

Jesus ran into the same thing. He said:

> *Oh, Jerusalem, Jerusalem, murderer of the Prophets and stoner of those who are sent to her. How often I have wanted to gather your children, just as a hen gathers her chickens under her wings, and yet, you would not.*

There he was saying he just wanted to help, but the hierarchy of the churches didn't want his teachings. He could have walked through the streets of the Holy Land, blessing those who were around, but they didn't want it. It doesn't mean the Spirit was any less present. The Spirit was the same then and yesterday as It is today and forevermore. The Spirit fully *is*. The Spirit, Thing Itself, is full present. It's not as if we can tell God how to do something or how to create something. It is all created. All possibility exists! Right where you are, you bring about the healing, the fullness, the abundance, the love and the success within your life as you recognize and acknowledge that it comes through your consciousness.

Just as an artist brings forth what it is he feels and hears inside himself, an architect brings forth all the details on a drafting table or computer—because it is inside them. All that is necessary for your life is within your consciousness. It's not as if we're telling God what to do to bring it forth. It is already. Have you got what I'm saying? The truth *is*. It is this simple.

Usurp God's Position Lately?

One thing I've noticed throughout my years in the Ministry is people like to usurp God's position. It sounds kind of farfetched, but I listen to people in their prayers, telling God how to do it. I listen to people talk with God and tell God how it should be. Fly with Spirit and remember the presence of God, and that God knows how to do it, whatever "it" is. God knows how to do it for you in a very good and grand and glorious way, but you've got to give God a chance. You've got to allow It to intercede. You've got to allow It to have its interception within your experience.

Billy Graham shared an interesting story about a celebrated neurologist in Philadelphia by the name of Dr. S.W. Mitchell. Coming home from an extra-long day, exhausted and ready to go to sleep, he had just gotten into bed when he heard a knock on his door. Getting up, he answered the door and found a little girl standing there, who said, "My mom is very sick. She needs your help. Come quick." Although exhausted, as a doctor he was compelled to go, so he pulled on his coat and followed the little girl. It was a cold, blustery, wintry, snowy night. He found the mother shivering with pneumonia, and secured the medical assistance she needed to get her out of there and into a warm, dry hospital. Once everything was secure, Dr. Mitchell said to the mother, "Wow, you sure have a very responsible and intelligent little girl who's able to take care of you like that." Startled, the mother looked up and said, "My little girl died a month ago. Her coat and shoes are still hanging in the closet." Dr. Mitchell went to the closet, opened the door and there was the very coat, hanging there dry, that the little girl had worn when she'd come to his door that night.

How do these things happen? I don't know. When you start dealing in the realm of consciousness and in the spiritual realm, the how isn't always easy to explain, nor is it important. I'm telling you, don't try to usurp God's power. Spirit or Life can figure things out in ways we know not of. All we must do is recognize God. Let's begin to drop our concepts of God and allow ourselves to become a transparency for the presence of God. You don't have to become a wizard when it comes to knowing all the different techniques. It's not about praying on one foot or sticking your finger in your ear and jumping up and down and chanting the right words. It is simply recognizing God. Fly in Spirit and whatever you are working on during the day, during lunch, during the night, do it with God. Keep bringing your awareness back to this place. Drop your concept of what you think Spirit is, because all I really know is that God *is*. Can you trust this flow? As soon as I try to say It's "this" (whatever "this" is) I get into the finite form. I can't tell you where It is. I can't tell you really what It is. All we really know as healers and spiritual people is God *is* and that "isness" is everywhere.

What Do You Recognize?

The very first step to prayer is recognition of God—recognition of that Power, the Life Force, and the Love. It is a recognition of that Spirit that is surrounding us in our lives. When things don't seem to shift immediately for what seems to be our betterment, let's remember *God is still there.*

There have been times when I've been flying that I've had to put the plane down in areas I had not planned on because of weather or running low on fuel. As a result of these unexpected landings, I've found some of the greatest people and resting places, so much so that the stop turned out to be the highlight of my trip. In thinking it has to show up a certain way we run the risk of closing down to creativity. This happens when we hold onto our rap—you know: "I'm looking for this perfect relationship, Mr. or Ms. Right, and it has to show up at this singles club that I've paid $40 to go and experience"—or whatever your story is.

I remember a gentleman in one of my churches, who once lived in the obscure jungles of Costa Rica, where it seemed there was no possible way you could find him. While traveling, another woman from my church was out on a tour of the jungle down there and somehow met up with him and it turned into true love. It's amazing how this unfolded, going beyond the concept of how it's supposed to be. It was Spirit in action, and definitely could not have been planned by a human mind.

Expanding the Peripheral Vision

Joseph Campbell wrote, "When you are no longer compelled by desire or fear, when you have seen the radiance of eternity in all the forms of time, when you follow your bliss, doors will open where you would not have thought they were. The world will step in and help." That's exciting to think about. In order to come to this place of fearlessness, we must expand our view of what's possible, to see and be aware of ever greater vistas and realms of possibility. Truly, in a place of this expanded vision that comes with our trusting the flow, we are able to look within ourselves and at all that surrounds us and view the infinite and eternal.

When you're looking for that new whatever-it-is you might be looking for and you start practicing this connection with Source, dropping your attachment to the way things are supposed to look, things start going pretty well in your world. Sometime one might start thinking, "Wow, I'm hot stuff." It's the height of egotism to think you're the one who is doing these things. You've now got a new rap going; you've got a new story: "Boy, I'm all powerful. Look at these healings I can now do because I've got the basic principles down." If we start saying, "I'm so benevolent, I'm so good, I'm so generous," that is the ego speaking. Let's not lose sight that these healings—the good, the generosity, the benevolence, the love—is the activity of Spirit moving through you. Do you understand the difference? It's important. Because when you move into the flow and all of a sudden life begins to work in wonderful ways, it is essential for you not to lose sight that it is God moving through you, causing you to find good coming to you from your friends, your family and people around you. God is the Source. You are not the Source—Spirit is the Source. As Joseph Campbell is telling us, those doors will open up and life will help us. We can end up in the obscure jungles of Costa Rica and find the amazing soul mate, the only one on the planet, in a way we would never have thought of, if we are willing to let go of the negativity, the doubt, and step into a place of trust and recognition of the presence of God.

When something does tend to go amiss and you're blown off your flight course, don't take it too personally—expand your vision. If you were growing a garden and for some reason your let-

123

tuce wasn't growing very well one month, you wouldn't go out and get mad at the lettuce seed. Maybe it's not getting enough sun, or maybe it's getting too much water, or maybe it needs more fertilizer. You'd attempt to understand the situation, not get ticked off at the seed. But when something goes amiss in our lives, too often we attempt to blame. We'll point a finger at a person or a thing, as opposed to attempting to understand what needs to be worked out so we can be part of the natural expression, that seed within us—the God presence that wants to grow and blossom. We have to get out of blame, and give up the negativity that impedes the creativity of God from showing up in our lives—because God wants to show up. It really does.

Dueling With God?

Are you dueling with God these days? Five words: *God is the only supply.* That's it. There is no other place. It is essential to get rid of dualistic thinking. If you want to get rid of the wants in your life, stop dueling with God and begin to embrace the allness, the fullness. Just choose to trust and experience It showing up in your life. God doesn't care where It shows up, so use your peripheral vision to spot Spirit.

Let's use this expanded vision in our lives and say, "What can I do? What am I willing to do?" If you're one to turn off, saying, "I don't want to hear this," it's time to take a look inside of yourself and see where you are denying the Flow into your life. Where are you putting the Power? There is a Power—a great Power. It is a Power for good greater than we are and we can use It and It can use us. How are you using the Power? You are using it. Are you creating tough times in your world? I want you to know there is nobody out there to get you. Are you looking for employment?

Employment is available right now. People say, "Well, it's tough. We're in the valleys." Well, the valleys are where transformation takes place. These tough times are education for the intellect to know the soul. When you're down in it, you get to see very up close and clear. It's when you're up high that everything looks very small. When society is going through a recession or a tough time, individuals have wonderful opportunities to prosper. When society is going through a tough economy, fresh ideas just pop up and businesses can double in size—the environment is ripe. But if you want to believe that you are not being supported by life, go ahead. Complain. Grumble. But do something about it! Have the courage to create in your world, because there's a Flow. You've got to trust the Flow. You've got to trust that It is there.

People choose to look for places to blame—society, the world, friends or something else. "That's why things aren't working," they accuse. "That's how I got into this predicament," they maintain, shrinking from accountability. They are so busy looking for why things are messed up in their lives that they'll claim they happened because of a childhood, or because of a past-life experience. Who knows why they happen? But I'll tell you, to move past them you may shrink the accountability to yourself, look within yourself. It makes it a lot simpler. Instead of going out there in the world trying to figure it out, it saves you a lot of time if you just say, "Okay, I'm accountable for this predicament in my life. I'm going to have the courage to create my intention. I'm going to let go of the how-to's. I'm going to trust God, who's bigger than I am, to figure it out. I'm going to take the accountability." In taking accountability for the challenges or predicaments that you're in comes the amazing thing called freedom to recreate. When you've given your power away to something outside, then you're prone to a victim mentality. When you're giving your power away to something outside, you're seeing some error out there in the world, and you're trying to figure it all out. If you have reclaimed your power, then comes the ability to recreate your world and experience with the intention, but you must have the courage to do this. You must have the courage to use the peripheral vision and catch a glimpse of God.

Not long ago, I had the opportunity to have lunch with my cousin who just moved to California from Minnesota. She's 18 or 19 and a freshman at the University of San Diego. She called me Thursday night to confirm that we could get together, and left directions on my voicemail. She spoke swiftly and I had some questions, so I called her the next morning before I came into work. She was still sleeping and couldn't quite get to the phone, so I followed what I thought were her directions to our meeting place. I didn't know the San Diego, Old Town area very well at the time, and I got a little confused. I was supposed to find her standing in front of the "white building on the left-hand side," but I discovered that all the buildings on the left-hand side were white. If I had come in the other driveway, all the buildings on the other side would have been on my left-hand side and they were also all white. I didn't really want to pass blame, but I did attempt to point out to her the discrepancy or the challenge in her directions. Interestingly enough, she didn't take any blame for it. She didn't take any responsibility. She listened as if to say, "Oh, that's interesting, Christian. Good story," and I was left with a clear sense that she absolutely did not unify with the blame. Her life was not heavier; her life was not impacted. I sat there thinking, "Wow, that's a really interesting approach to being and doing life." What a great way to keep our hearts open with friends, with young ones, with old ones, with everyone—not looking for mistakes, not looking to criticize, condemn or point any fingers, but rather just flying in love, trusting the flow of life.

A woman who had cancer worked quite a bit with the doctors and the medical treatments. Finally the doctor said there was nothing left that they could do. She remembered her son who was involved with Religious Science, and she thought maybe she would try his holistic approach to things. "Since the medical world can't do anything for me any more," she decided, "I'm going to try something else." She let go of those fake boundaries, those un-Godlike boundaries of the mind that say healing has to come through some particular medical treatment. After all, when it doesn't work, a person can either die or choose again. She chose again and she's still living to talk about it.

A wonderful friend and mentor of mine, Dr. Fletcher Harding, was given about a month to live. He had cancer throughout his bones and the medical community was convinced there was no way he could recover, yet he beat the cancer and experienced a complete remission. He shared with me that he'd never see his body as being sick, only as a perfectly healthy body doing what a sick mind tells it to do. We can heal our lives physically when we trust the Divine flow.

There is a lot of power in the word. The word is what sets the subjective in motion. If we were to stop making God have to fight through the garbage of our minds, can you imagine what this free-flowing power would manifest in our world? Yet we make the Life Force have to come through the turmoil, fears, anger, resentment and all sorts of stuff in order to show up in our lives. This Flow has got some maneuvering to do before It ever can actually come in for a straight landing. It's amazing It ever makes it through the emotional whirlwind. Imagine the remarkable things that would happen if we were just open and receptive, in a place of peace and believing, just trusting the Flow.

Not by Might

You can't wait around for God to do something because God already is doing something. This Flow exists when you are opening up to love, to God and not telling God how to do it or make your life better. You're not seeking anything; you're not telling God to do anything. You're just opening up to the grace of God, which is the peace, the love, and the well-being of our nature. Doing this, you'll come to know the truth and this truth is what sets you free. What are you going to serve: the truth, God or mammon? Mammon is of this world. We're talking about the Kingdom that is of another world. This world is where the struggle, the strife and the competition exist. In "thy Kingdom that is not of this world," we don't get around with might and power, but by grace, by peace and by trusting Spirit. Does this feel right? That's the knowingness of your heart that feels right inside. Your heart knows; it's the authentic compass. As we begin to look at focusing on Spirit, we move into the Omnipotence, which means the "all power." When we are in this Omnipotence place, the all power, then the sin, or the disease, or the lack, or whatever other stuff of this world that has raised its head in our experiences from time to time (which comes from dealing with two powers) begins to fade away. There isn't room for another power.

A lot of times I listen to people who are new in the New Thought movement, running around saying, "There is no evil; there is no sin; there is no sickness; there is no lack." Well, in this physical world there is. There is evil stuff happening on this planet. There is suffering going on here, but this is the key to making the statement true: When we are in the presence of

God, when we are in that Divine realization, that Omnipotence, there is no other power.

Spirit knows how to show up in your life. Don't belittle God and think you have to tell God how to do it. A lot of times people say, "Okay, Christian says I'm not to tell God how to do something, so maybe I'll just sit back and do nothing. You know, that meditative thing that's kind of good, you just kind of hang out." There's a balance here that is essential!

What tends to happen with many people within our society is they allow their minds to go into a dulled state of inertia. They allow themselves to work in a place that is not stimulating. They are more comfortable following policies, procedures and bylaws than they are adhering to the principle within their own lives. It is a lot easier to follow the status quo and that which is outlined in the dogma or creeds of an organization than it is to unify with Spirit and to know the principle of truth that is within your life. Jesus never said, "Let me check to see what the bylaws say." In rough and challenging periods, which do show up in our world sometimes, when the rules are not in the book on how to do it, adhering to principle by listening to your integrity through your connection with God because you are flying with Spirit, you are able to know what to do.

I keep a flashlight in my flight bag to help me read my maps at night. I hadn't used it in a year, so before an upcoming night flight, I checked to see if it was working. The battery had been brand-new when I stuck it in there, but when I turned on the flashlight, nothing happened. It didn't work. I opened it up and the battery was stuck. I shook it out and it was corroded. The battery acid had come out. That brand-new battery had gone bad because it had never been used. Trust, faith, love or any spiritual principle operates under the same law: Use it or lose it. What you have, which is infinite in its possibilities, will become corroded if it's stored away in darkness and never used in your life.

You have to use these principles or your life will reflect the corrosion caused by the apathy of not doing, or by living in question or fear. It takes guts to step out into this place, trusting life, experiencing those vulnerable spots in you that you really didn't want to have to deal with in this lifetime.

Recently I sat in a great state of gratitude as Seaside opened its doors to the homeless and fed many people in the community. As part of the Flow of this particular project, one of the wonderful things that transpired happened the day before when we had the sanctuary lined up with 100 seats. A bunch of elementary school girls wearing their Brownie uniforms came in. They were just giggling and having the best time being part of the community, setting up the tables and decorations and the pumpkins. Hearing this kind of childlike laughter going on in the room, I just sat in a state of gratitude, saying, "Thank you, God. Thank you that Seaside is part of the flow." There's such gratitude to be found in the recognition of those things that just begin to naturally unfold. It's letting go of the ego, the forcing, the trying to make it happen—it's releasing.

After the first step of a *recognition* of God, our second step is *unification* with It. If God is all things, I am one with Spirit, and being in that place of oneness, we are able to *realize* the spiritual truth. I mean this is just the natural state in which we have learned to enunciate, so we can understand how the spoken word moves through us. It's the recognition; it's the unification. Being one with Spirit, you realize the truth from this perspective. Once you come to the realization and see as God sees, you are filled with gratitude. That is a prosperous state of being, knowing from God's perspective it's done. It's being able to say, "Thank you, it's done," instead of, "Oh no, will it happen? When will it happen?" Rather, knowing it's done, you let it go.

Spirit shows up in a practical way within our lives. If we were lost in the woods with no food, as Elijah was, the ravens or the birds could deliver food, or we could find cakes baking on the stone, or, as with Moses, manna could drop out of the sky. Spirit knows how to take care of us. It is practical living when we can let go of our outlining, and our way of telling God how to do it, and instead realize the beauty that is, right where we are, and be grateful for it! With such gratitude we are in richness, not in a place of scarcity or lack, but rather in the fullness of God. From this place you are able to fly through life, radiating out the light that you are, and which Spirit is. If you are looking for employment, Spirit then shows up as an employer. If you need some financial influx, God is all things, and It shows up in the appropriate way. You don't need to pray to God to bring you some money. What is essential is to know God is. What a joy God is. It is. We are living within this Presence. All the finding or financing that you could ever want or need is. It is right here right now. Release your concepts of having to get to it. Release any of the human thinking that says, "God, you've got to show up to help me out of this one." Let's let go of this and allow ourselves to be lifted up to that higher place. Let us fly within the Spirit. Let us experience the power of the word.

I listened to a race-boat driver share an experience of a crash he had. He said he was going along the water at absolute top speed, pushing his boat to the limit. He was at a bit of an angle, in a little precarious position, out of alignment with the flow of the power. He hit a small ripple in the surface of the water, and his boat went flying into the air and spun a zillion times. Ejected out of his boat, he landed so far down into the water he didn't know which way was up. You can talk to any surfer—it happens to us all the time, but this guy at least had a vest on. He said in the midst of the panic, not knowing which way was up, which way was down or which way was sideways, what he had to do was calm himself long enough, quiet his mind, release his struggle to get back to the surface, and allow his vest to lift him back up to the surface. If we can quiet our minds enough, the Spirit will then begin to lift us above the crashes and the difficulties. We will begin to feel the Kingdom of Heaven that is within our lives.

Back Down or Back Up

While Kalli and I had been skiing for several days on our Whistler, Canada, trip, our legs were tired, so we decided to take a day off and go snowmobiling. We went to an absolutely beautiful place and rented snowmobiles. I didn't know where we were headed or what was beyond where we were. We just kept heading toward the beauty, off on a forest highway of snow, going higher and higher. We were in a clouded area for quite a while, when all of a sudden we went about the clouds into the pristine, white mountains scattered with snow-flocked trees under blue sky. Racing around on alpine meadow was exhilarating, so when Kalli got off the snowmobile, I decided to go exploring even farther. Speeding across what I thought was a flat path, to my surprise I was catapulted over the edge of an embankment, burying the snowmobile in a riverbank and dumping me into the stream, down below. Yet I still knew I was in the presence of God. The guide, who had taken us out there, came and dug me out along with the snowmobile. Even though I noticed I was getting cold, I didn't really want to return. I kept looking beyond. I kept looking to God. We went up even higher and, unbeknownst to me, they had this wonderful mountain cabin nestled on a precipice, with gorgeous, expansive views. Here we were served a wonderful lunch and hot cider. Had I not been looking beyond, I would have probably decided to go back down below to dry out and warm up. But looking above and beyond to God, I discovered there was something even greater waiting for me, waiting for us.

Second Corinthians says, "Where the Spirit of the Lord is, there is liberty." When we are in Spirit and opening up to It, we are releasing our lower selves and saying, "Okay, God have your way with me. Okay, God, I am with you. I'm in the Presence. I am living in a state of gratitude. Lift me up. Reveal to me. Impart to me. Show me. Allow me to understand." But with our prayers we get into these affirmations as if we are attempting to create God. We get into making and declaring these statements of truth, as if our declaring of truth is what makes it true. That's not true. What is true is—It is. Let's begin to allow the word to impart itself so we are speaking the truth, not attempting to make the truth come true, but becoming the mouthpiece through which the truth is speaking. This is releasing yourself. This is releasing your mind, your fears and your concerns. So what comes forth from you is the word of God and it allows you to get into the rhythm of Divine living. It allows you to fly in the power of Spirit. It gets us out of the human living. The human world is where we end up with stress and anxiety, with broken hearts and with all the different kinds of "isms" and diseases that the medical world wants us to believe are the truth because they are showing up in your body.

I read last year there were one million heart attacks in the United States; there were thirteen billion doses of tranquilizers and barbiturates passed out; there were eight million stomach ulcers related to stress and fifty thousand suicides; one out of eight suicide attempts were successful; and there are reported to be twelve million alcoholics within the U.S. this last year. (I think that is a low number.) These were the recent staggering statistics released! I think the stress and challenges come from a result of false importance we put on our problems. We magnify them as if the world is not going to make it if I don't get this, if I don't understand, if I don't meet this deadline, the planet is not going to go on, so I'll have an ulcer over it. I'll stress out and hold the weight of my world upon my shoulders to get it through. Give it up! Let it go! You'll find that you can both soar to new heights and come in for smooth, timely landings, too.

This is also the way healing happens—by letting go. It doesn't happen by putting things together and telling God how to do it, because prayer is not telling God how to do it. Prayer is listening. It's God that has the power. God is the power. It is the Presence that heals. So how is it that we can speak our word and sometimes it doesn't seem to happen? We tell the storms to cease and they don't listen—the lightning and thunder keep going. We tell the waves to still and they seem to pick up their momentum. Yet God says, "Let there be light," and—BOOM—we have a sun. Spirit speaks, saying, "Pick up your bed and walk," and one can walk. It is the Spirit of God that can speak through you, but you must be willing to let go and allow the Spirit to speak. It's not petitioning Spirit. It's not making God do anything; rather, it's quieting our mind enough, our ego, our humanness enough so we can release all of our stuff and allow the words we speak to be the Presence of God. Those words that are spoken are released into the law.

Having taken off on this powerful flight in Spirit, this power of prayer, we have *recognized* the Presence in the midst of confusion, and *unified* with the beauty, with that love, with that wholeness. From that place of recognizing the essence and knowing the "I am-ness" of it we are able to *realize* the beauty of the flowers, the beauty of the "I am"—the beauty that you are. From that place of realization of the spiritual truth of any situation you might be looking at, you're filled with a sense of *gratitude*, because you're not looking for it to happen. It has happened. It is established. It is the Presence of God, and being that it is done, you let go. You don't hold on to it. You don't keep digging up the ground to see if the lettuce is bigger now. It is. The last step of this powerful flight with Spirit is to *release* that which you have seen and known, that which you have spoken. As you release it, you begin to open up the floodgates and health, wealth, abundance and the fullness of God pours forth into your life. This is what happens when you trust the flow.

CHAPTER EIGHT

JET STREAM OF ABUNDANCE

*Inside myself, I've noticed a
growing desire, almost a mandate from
Spirit, to reveal to people around me that
they are already prosperous; the
abundance of God is right where they
are. Right where you are, God is. It's
about rightful seeing, seeing rightly—
seeing the presence is here and not
worrying about hoarding and holding
on. When we're holding on, then we're
into a place of trying to persevere. We're
afraid somebody's going to get it from us,
thinking, "There is only so much to go
around and I've got to hold on to my
part." This is survival. To get out of it
you must free your mind and know you
are part of the wonderful flow of Spirit.*

"So, I hear you're going to buy a plane," an acquaintance commented, his expression one of curiosity mingled with suspicion of my good judgment. It wasn't the first time I'd been faced with the subject since finally earning my pilot's license and deciding to buy my own plane.

"That's right," I answered with a confident smile.

"Has to be expensive," he said, almost too casually.

Certain he was fishing for an explanation (for some strange reason, I'd discovered that some people wondered how I could afford a plane on a minister's salary), I offered, "Well, I found one for no money out of my pocket." Feeling a bit embarrassed, as if I had to justify my purchase, I went on, "The previous owner is carrying some paper and taking some of the payment in flight time, and I'll make payments by renting out the plane." I had it all figured out—how it would save me time and money on my travels, all the good works it would free me up to do—I could explain it all to anyone who asked. Apparently I convinced him.

"Great deal," he responded, now sounding less skeptical.

I felt funny with people thinking I was affluent enough to afford my own airplane. After all, I didn't want to appear greedy or pretentious. There are preconceived perspectives the collective consciousness places on someone who goes out and buys a plane.

As I connected with Spirit I knew I didn't need to come up with reasons or excuses. There will always be people who have their personal scarcity issues and will attempt to pull others down into limitation. We live in a universe of abundance and it took absolutely nothing away from the universe for me to buy a plane. As children of God, abundance is our birthright, and I own and enjoy my plane today.

I love talking, writing and reading about abundance, because my world always tends to reflect whatever it is I'm working on. I enjoy stepping into the abundant jet stream of Spirit, the powerful force constantly flowing above the lower world. The power of increase means catching the current of Spirit, being swept along in the powerful stream of abundance by participating in the giving and receiving of the Divine. This giving isn't done because it's an act you are supposed to do, or because "the principle says to do it, so I'm doing it." This giving is about the feeling behind it—not writing a check once a month to the starving kids of wherever (although this is good to do). Its essence and importance isn't in going through the routine or the ritual, it's being in the flow of the Presence. Spiritual wealth and spiritual abundance is a consciousness, which means being in this jet stream of life. It is becoming a channel through which the flow pours in and naturally pours out. If you dam up the outflow, there's a messy explosion. If you give with no inflow you dry up, and that's not pretty.

Clergyman Henry Ward Beecher said, "It is the heart that makes a man rich. He is rich according to what he is, not according to what he does." We are rich by what we are, which is God, so if you think you are your things and titles, then you're denying this truth. If what you are is a conduit for Source, then you are rich in Spirit. When you're giving from Source, you're not taking from your capital or principle but from a renewing, enhancing, vital channel of the flow. In the Bible, when the widow was asked to feed the prophet, it would've been impossible from the little she had. Yet she became a channel of the infinite flow, which left her with more than she had when she started.

One Sunday morning at 3:30, when I was up doing my regular meditation and preparing for service, I got this insight on prayer. We do our prayers and talk about "my" source, "my" abundance or "my" wealth, and I realized as long as it is "mine," there's a limitation to it. There's a separation to it. If we can know everybody's wealth and abundance, and the abundance that is, when we're not making it finite; we are realizing the infinite.

After having this insight, I took a look at a prayer I had written on prosperity. It said, "...my source, my good..." We talk about the sun and don't say "my sun," do we? "The rain falls on the just and the unjust, on the saint and the sinner," as the Bible says. This is the way wealth and abundance is. If we can get rid of "my abundance and my wealth," and just know that abundance is and we have entered this flow, the motion of this jet stream will naturally bring God's grace upon our world.

I'm really against poverty. Poverty is a disease, an abomination to the human soul. It's just not a very god thing. Can you agree with this? Poverty is a consciousness, and those who are into that kind of experience attempt to convince you of its truth. We must quiet the wants and get out of the place of survival. Our culture has been trained in consumption, keeping us low to the ground. The surface winds are always running into mountains and obstacles in their path, distorting and disturbing their direction and flow. We walk around saying, "I want this. I want that." Maybe not you, but then again, maybe, just occasionally, the material kind of person raises his head—the shopping maniac ready to go out there with this voracious appetite, hungry to devour something, anything he can find. Just as you are able to calm this down, it comes to your house via volumes of mail-order catalogs, enticing and teasing you. In our western culture we've been taught about acquisition and looking good. We've been indoctrinated into these ways of thinking.

Inside myself, I've notice a growing desire, almost a mandate from Spirit, to reveal to people around me that they are already prosperous, the abundance of God is right where they are. Right where you are, God is. It's about rightful seeing, seeing rightly— seeing the presence is here and not worrying about hoarding and holding on. When we're holding on, we're into a place of trying to persevere. We're afraid somebody's going to get it from us, thinking, "There is only so much to go around and I've got to hold on to my part." This is survival. To get out of it you must free your

mind and know you are part of the wonderful flow of Spirit. Trust
the continual replenishing process.

Zen of Abundance

In ancient China, they used to really honor the artists and
craftsmen who did things that brought out the best of whatever
it was that they were working on. The old Taoist philosophy in
Japan led to an offshoot called Zen, which can't be taught and
can only be experienced. Zen was about being part of the order
and the flow. It was about those individuals who could attune
themselves with whatever it was on which they were working. It
didn't only include working on the spiritual; it included whatever
one was working on. If you were a gardener, this would mean
being in tune with the Spirit and giving your absolute best and
receiving from the Spirit the guidance and direction to develop
your gardening. A master potter would give of himself to create a
piece of pottery, which may not look physically perfect, yet had a
magical aura about it. Have you ever seen a piece of art that wasn't
quite perfect, yet there was a spirit to it that moved your soul? It
was those individuals who got in touch with the flow. They gave
of themselves in all their work. This is how increase and abundance show up in your world. It's the "power of increase"—giving
yourself fully to what you are doing—the Zen, this flow, being
powered along by the jet stream of abundance, which carries you
to the ideal destination.

The key is the flow of Spirit in all areas of your life. Do all areas
of your life reflect abundance? What about your surroundings?
I'm not talking about a nice house sitting on the bluff, overlooking the ocean. It's not necessary to own one of those to be into
abundance. What I'm asking is: Does your environment reflect

order? Do you have mounds of junk all over reminding you that you don't have time to deal with it? You "don't have time"? Look at what goes into your subjective. Or do you have a leaky faucet that drips, drips, drips—"don't have, don't have"—and you think, "Well, I'll get around to calling a plumber. I don't really want to spend the money." Whatever the thinking is behind your inactivity, it pulls you into the lower realm of the surface winds. What flow are you into? What about the car? Does it have any dents or scratches in it? Every time you go to your car you see this old ding and think, "Oh gosh, I've got to get it fixed. I just haven't got the money right now (or haven't got the time, or it been inconvenient)." Whatever the reasoning, every time you open the door it reminds you of not having. When I'm talking about environment, this is what I mean. You could be living in the lowest part of town, but if the world around you is elegant, if the world around you reminds you of the magnificence of your being, then it's empowering, which means it is abundance. This is the power of increase, when you are part of the flow of Spirit giving to you and receiving from you.

Are the things around you reminding you of the power? What is it you want in your world? What is it you would like to create? People go through the ritual of writing a check or writing their goals, or taking the workshops, but if the environment around you is not part of the flow of Spirit that is giving to you, sourcing you, you're missing out on the power of the jet stream of abundance. You don't have to know how to create in your world. That's not your job. What a relief! It's good news! You don't have to know how, you just have to know what. There's a cliché: "Your subjective takes the cues and gives you the how-to's." But those who like control in their world find this a difficult concept to grasp.

It's as though God were the pilot of a large passenger jet. You get in the airliner and if you could just sit and relax—no problem. Spirit, the Pilot, God knows how to get you to your chosen destination. But the challenge usually shows up the minute you decide you want to get on the jet, go to the ticket window, try to order a ticket, then vacillate, "Do I want to go here or do I want to go there?" They can give you the ticket, but you're debating here-or-there. How can Spirit fill this kind of request? You're not yet part of the flow. You're trying to check it out—"Should I jump in? Shouldn't I?"—running hot, running cold. Then you get your ticket and you get on the jet and what do you want to do? You want to take the controls away from the Pilot. "Let me show you how to fly. I know the shortest, quickest, most direct route, how to miss all the turbulence." My goodness, what we do to keep ourselves into stress, struggle and resistance.

Increasing Up or Down?

God already is. God has already given it all, so you can't wait for God to give it to you now. What is essential is to get rid of that which impairs you from rising into the Power of the jet stream. You've got to have the courage. I watch people buy into the fears, the worries. They'll sit down and tell me what's stopping them from going forward in life. "Let me tell you why I can't make this work. Let me tell you why there are other people who do it for less money...I'm too old...too young...too weak or strong...not educated enough." They come forth with such vivid, imagined, false boundaries of mind as to why they can't do it that they remain grounded. They talk a good talk, saying, "Yes, I could create my own reality..." yet they are sitting there starving, living their self-generated fears.

The positive power of increase is about being one with the jet stream, the powerful flow of Spirit. You've got the whole universe flowing, moving right into the vortex of the funnel of where you are. You are at the funnel, this is the power, yet we cut it off by saying, "Hey, God, I'll take care of it." Spirit knows the way. It's beyond you. If you can really believe this, you're going to watch miraculous things begin to manifest as your life. The depth of creation will be profound. The ways it will show up in your world will be routes you would never for a moment have imagined. You've got to trust and believe.

I remember reading a story about how a town stepped into the jet stream of love and abundance when one of their young girls was battling cancer. This young girl was going to the town's annual livestock sale, wondering whether or not to sell her shaggy, funny-looking little lamb. As a result of her battle with cancer, for months she had seen only the inside of hospitals, dealing with a wide range of medical treatments. This would be her first day out into the outside world, and she seriously debated whether or not she wanted to sell her lamb, yet she really wanted to do what she could to help out her parents. The lambs were bringing in a couple of dollars a pound, so she decided she was willing to do it, and she went to the center of the ring to set up her lamb for everybody to see.

Inspired in the moment, the auctioneer told the people in the audience what the young owner of the lamb was going through. The results of what took place after that were amazing. The bidding started coming in and she sold her lamb for more than 15 dollars a pound. But it didn't end there. The person who bought the lamb paid and then gave her the lamb back, and they sold it again, and they gave it back, and they sold it again and again. After that, all you could hear was the crowd shouting, "Resell!

Resell!" The people in this town were getting together and making bids on this lamb and giving it back, but when the businesses started bidding, the money really started showing up! After three dozen sales, they had raised over 16,000 dollars to pay off some of the medical expenses she had incurred, and she got to go home with her little lamb that day.

Just look at the power here. The many ways of God are unknown. Those ideas are the power of God in action. If you want to experience the increase, the jet stream of abundance, you have to fly above what you've known. You also have to give; this is how you open the throttle to power the lift. You have to be willing to open. I truly believe people have goodness inside of them, because It's God. I watch experiences like this young girl's awaken in individuals their aliveness, their goodness, their passion and desire to be givers in life. Everyone went home feeling good that day.

We miss out on so much in life because of apathy. We miss out on so much because we forget to ask for it. WE FORGET TO ASK. God is unlimited and yet, we have limited ourselves with this Divine experience. Is God unlimited? You bet God is! We're the ones who put the limit on our God. We're the ones who have juggled around in the world trying to rearrange ourselves so we can receive goodness from Spirit. It's like trying to take the controls from the Pilot, as opposed to allowing ourselves to be swept along by higher velocities of the jet stream.

The Prodding Thorns

Do you have some clothes in the closet you are saving for the "right occasion"? What about the fine china you save only for a special occasion? Are you not special enough to dine on the best all the time? Yes, you are! Are you not entitled to put on your best clothes and walk out feeling great? When you put on good clothes, don't you feel good? This is how you affirm abundance. This is how you get out of your wants—you start enjoying what is in your life now. Now is the time. Now! Spirit wants to flow, wants to carry you along in the jet stream of abundance. Are you grateful for the good in your world now? If someone gave you a gaudy, fluorescent muumuu would you be able to say thank you, or would you sit in judgment of the gift? The sense of gratitude and appreciation is what the jet stream currents are made of.

I remember this one gentleman sharing how he was going to start practicing tithing, giving back ten percent to the church in his life. He decided he wanted more in his world, so he thought it would be a good idea to practice what he feared, which was letting go of the money he valued in his world. He was going to practice the principle of circulating by giving back to one of his spiritual sources. He began doing this, and six weeks into his practice he lost his job as an engineer. Saying thank you was nowhere near the top of his list of reactions. I remember him adamantly questioning me, "Christian, why isn't this working?" But his decision to practice the principle was not based upon its working; it was based upon his commitment to Spirit. It was based upon the principles and a faith that didn't depend on outside conditions. The first month of being unemployed, part of his time was hell and part of it was happiness, based on whether he was in trust or fear. Quickly he got back to a place where he decided to keep giving, to keep practicing, to keep having the faith. He'd been let go from the aerospace industry and was given two months' severance pay. At the end of the first month, a private electronic company hired him and he was making twice his previous salary. This happened because he kept the faith; he chose to believe. This faith was not based upon outside conditions having to look a certain way. Any thorns in our nests of comfort are proddings, which indicate it's time for us to leap out and discover our spiritual wings—time to discover we are greater than any of those previous conditions, while getting away from our prejudices in thinking it has to be a certain way.

A rabbi shared a story about someone asking him if they should save the best grapes till last when eating them. The rabbi told him to eat the best grapes first, so as to always be eating the best grapes. If you start enjoying the best you have now, then you will always be enjoying the best! You'll be getting out of the place of want. You won't be into a place of survival—"Oh God, help me and bail me out of it this time (whatever it would be)." Harmonious prospering is a key. It's not simply about creating success, because the flip side of success is failure. If you're not trying to create success, but you are choosing to be harmoniously prosperous, you're just choosing to be part of the abundant flow of the jet stream—if you give up the struggle.

We've been trained in struggle. We are trained to study lack or disease. Do you realize how much research has been put into studying disease? Do you know how many people can tell you how they are unable to pay their bills? People study how long they can make it before things run out and believe it is by the sweat of their brow that they are going to make it—and only if they work hard enough. Nose to the grindstone, they are using their energy and their know-how, and forgetting about the infinite flow. It is like Sisyphus, who was eternally damned to roll a stone to the top of a hill. He would get the stone just about to the top of the hill and down it would come again. He'd roll it back up and down it would come—and the story goes on and on. Well, materialism is like this. With materialism, you think you can acquire and get enough—but just as you get there, down it comes again. You're afraid of losing, afraid somebody will take it from you, or someone will have one up on you, so what you have worked so hard to accumulate now keeps you bound to this way of being, to protecting your asset or piece of property or whatever it is, and keeps you working to pay those credit card bills. All of a sudden, something other than Spirit is accepting your awareness. Remember the commandment, "Thou shalt put no other gods before me?" People start concerning themselves with bills, studying scarcity, disliking mailboxes for the bills they hold, plotting how they are going to pay them. The mind becomes preoccupied with thoughts other than God. The golden calf has now taken form.

Spirit is infinite. It is not bound; It is limitless. And what are you? Spirit! The truth of your being is limitless. Who has put the caps or limits on your state of being in this human form? You have. Who is going to remove it? You are. The way you do this is to start living from the inside. People get stuck by living in the world of phenomena. They're living in a world "out there." It is time to move inside, to look inside instead of outside—it's that simple. This is where the Spirit is and the turbo charge kicks in.

I Shall Not Want

Remember the first line of the Twenty-third Psalm? "The Lord is my Shepherd, I shall not want." That's the key! When we know God, we shall not want. When we know the Infinite Presence, we shall not want! We will move to a higher altitude, a higher state of being, of realization and experience in our lives. But we're so trained in wanting because of things like those catalogs that show up in the mail saying, "You don't have one of these? How can you be a whole person when your jeans aren't tight enough?" and we believe it. It's amazing.

How are you giving? Even motivational speakers talk about giving. As a minister, I sometimes find myself a little apprehensive to talk about how important it is to give, because people will point fingers and say, "There goes the Reverend with his tithing stuff again." But it's absolutely true that it is essential for us to give in life. It is part of the flow of abundance. Man has talked about tithing and giving since the beginning of time. If it didn't work, they would have knocked it off by now, because there are enough people who don't like the concept. If there were any loopholes, I promise I would have found them by now. The regular systematic giving to what honors Spirit in your life will blast you along into the jet stream of abundance. Why ten percent? Perhaps simply because it's an easy number to figure out. You know the Power of One, the Unity and God, ten percent to God. It's a lot easier to calculate than 11.9 percent.

That ten percent is only the training wheels. It teaches us to regularly remember it is God who gives us the power to experience wealth in our lives. It's not our employer or the renters in whatever little house we own for our supplemental income. It is God, everywhere present, seeking to pour forth the abundance. If you realize you're the one who puts the caps on it, yet you want to experience more wealth in your life, it is essential to get into the consciousness of the abundant flow with Spirit by honoring Spirit in your life. This is why one gives back to their spiritual source, supporting a place where Spirit is showing Itself to them. It is essential to practice this regularly, so Spirit shows up in your life regularly. Why the dollars? Because we have a lot of energy on that stuff. It is also important to give as a volunteer in every area of our lives. You want to be an emanation of the Divine Energy. You want to be an emanation of the flow and an expression of Spirit.

That's a powerful prayer: "I am a Divine emanation. I am part of the abundant flow."

Metaphysically, I see people initially work with prayer on how to demonstrate "princes and palaces and parking spots" and other material kinds of things. In Religious Science, you get these "how-to's." In Science of Mind I, the Foundation Class, you learn how to manipulate the Law on how to create these things. But in truth, if you are praying to get something, you are coming from a place of "have not." God doesn't need our suggestions or advice. Spirit knows how to sustain and maintain Itself as you. We need to shift our thinking to know that "all is" and step into this place, the vortex of energy, and begin to feel and to recognize the motion of Spirit. Know your consciousness is the activity God is having. We must contemplate God's grace as our sufficiency. Realization is the demonstration.

People will say, "But my bills just keep coming in. They just keep showing up in my world." When it comes to paying bills, I invite you to make a ritual of it, a beautiful moment, a Divine experience: light a candle, notice that it's an energy exchange going on. When I go to write my checks, for me it's a ritual. The first thing I always do when paying my bills is write my check to God because it is God that gives us the Power to get wealth. Make it a spiritual experience. What are you exchanging your human energy for in life? If we're dealing with energy, aren't we told energy is infinite? If energy is infinite, then we are dealing with this energy exchange, we are dealing with an infinite source. If you have let go of the guarantees, the boundaries and fake constraints of your mind, you are allowing God the space to show up in your life in a powerful and expanding way. If you give your day doing the work you love, the dollars will appear to pay mortgages, car payments, food and whatever other expenditures you have. Isn't this an amazing spiritual exchange of energy?

Take a look at the back of all your dollar bills and read what's printed there. I don't care what dollar amount you use. What's in the back of them all? "In God we trust." Absolutely! It is in God we trust—not Uncle Sam, not our employer, not our relationship. It is God who moves through everyone as channels and when we can place our faith, our conviction upon the Higher Power, the Infinite Energy, we will find It manifests in ways that are great and wonderful. Your life will show it. It will make a difference in your world.

If a person were to take a hundred million gallons of water out of the ocean here in San Diego and drop it in the ocean in Monterey, what difference would it make to the ocean? Believing there is only one Divine and Abundant Energy to all things, it doesn't matter to Spirit where It shows up, because It's still everywhere. At the individual level, the choice becomes ours as to what degree one wants to experience this life. It doesn't matter to God if It shows up in San Diego, or if It shows up north of here. God is everywhere. We're talking about this infinite Sea, this infinite realm of possibilities, and if you move It from here to over there, it's irrelevant to Life. Prosperity, wealth, energy, joy, love, well-being—it doesn't matter in whose life or world It's showing up, because It's all in the universal sea already. If you want to get out of survival, start recognizing being part of the affluent flow.

Begin to be grateful. As long as you are into gratitude, you can't be into "want." You can't be into gratitude and want at the same time. Gratitude is a very prosperous place to be, because if you are grateful, what you are feeling and what you are experiencing is It already. Gratitude allows your thinking to shift to being filled with "greatness"—"grate-full." Gratitude allows you to step to the next level. Gratitude allows you to see rightly and to be filled with Spirit.

It's not about seeing things your way and being here to set those things right. It's about seeing it rightly. What gratitude does is allow you to see things rightly and if you are in this place of gratitude, you are out of the wants. If you are out of the wants, you are no longer into the place of survival. You might as well fly the jet stream of abundance and experience the givingness of God. There will no longer be a sense of lack or limitation in your world, because you will be living and experiencing the fullness of it all.

If you choose to dwell in the place of the Most High, the lower world of effect will be able to hitch a ride on your flight. The nature of God is fulfillment. Spirit is forever fulfilling Itself. Life cannot withhold itself from you, just as the jet stream must flow, it cannot decide it will stop midway and pick up again. God doesn't give today and tomorrow, and withhold the next day.

Let your thoughts be on the realization of Spirit fulfilling Itself and you will be lifted into the natural spiritual stream. Seek God with no other purpose than to seek God, and your whole heart and soul responds to the fullness that is. The jet stream goes before us and prepares the way. All will be provided for, when needed. It it's a plane, a plane will be there. If it's a car, a car will be there. Spirit dwells in all places—if it is money, or a relationship, if it is supply it shall be provided. Remember to seek Spirit, not things, and all will appear!

GAINING ALTITUDE – CHRIST CONSCIOUSNESS

I really like what Jesus said:
"Heaven and earth shall pass away,
but my word shall not, until it is
fulfilled." Now that's faith!
When we can have the consciousness
of this kind of faith, we're going to have
a lot of miracles in our lives.
We're going to have a lot of good
showing up in our world.
When we can have this kind of faith,
we're going to experience tremendous
transformations.
I believe this kind of faith
is very much attainable.
It's so simple a seven-year-old can get it,
yet it's so profound philosophers can't refute it.

Piloting my plane, I looked at the terrain up ahead and spotted the mountains drawing near. Knowing it was time to gain altitude in order to clear them, I glanced at my instruments and stated my ascent. As I soared over their majestic peaks from the safety of my vantage point, I viewed them with respect. Gaining altitude in order to assure safety was crucial. In fact, gaining altitude in order to maintain any sort of flight is crucial—otherwise you'd be flying into obstacles, which is not a good thing.

When flying through life, we'll find a need to gain altitude as well. Coming upon those mountains of challenges, we'll need to ascend to the higher atmosphere known as "Christ conscious-ness." The Bible says, "Awake, you who sleep, arise from the dead, and Christ will lead your life." This Christ leading you is not the person Jesus, but the Christ consciousness. Awake and arise—gain altitude—to this level of awareness, which will lead your life. Gaining this altitude means catching a glimpse of the God consciousness, knowing the mystical unity of Oneness. It is an altitude and an attitude that allows one to relax and be the Divine expression. Reaching these heights, you move naturally above those mountains of challenge, soaring from fear to faith.

In his book, *This Thing Called Life*, Ernest Holmes wrote, "...Jesus, walking through the multitude, diffused a healing power which touched into wholeness with its divine presence. His command stilled the wind and wave. His knowledge of spiri-tual law fed the thousands. His consciousness of peace calmed the troubled mind. His love was a healing balm to the sick. Jesus possessed the transcendent power...Jesus consciously brought the invisible power of Life to bear upon his environment...Jesus never claimed to be different from other men. He said: What I am you are also; what I do you can do...Did he not tell us that the kingdom of God is at hand? He told us that the only thing that obscured heaven is our lack of faith." This elevated consciousness, which manifests the invisible power of Life, is available to us all through faith.

It's wonderful the way love, well-being and good continue to show up in one's life when one continues to have faith. I really like what Jesus said: "Heaven and earth shall pass away, but my word shall not, until it is fulfilled." Now that's faith! When we can have the consciousness of this kind of faith, we're going to have a lot of miracles in our lives. We're going to have a lot of good showing up in our world. When we can have this kind of faith, we're going to experience tremendous transformations. I believe this kind of faith is very much attainable. It's so simple a seven-year-old can get it, yet it's so profound philosophers can't refute it. It is so demonstrable that scientific minds cannot repudiate it. It is so much of consciousness it can take one's psychological emotions to a transcendental state. It is so human that it can warm one's heart, taking one from a sense of loneliness to a place of light. This is the kind faith that is going to allow you to gain altitude over the Mt. Everests on your flight, or move the mountains or soar high above any cloud banks of challenges or turmoil.

What Are You Changing?

Our individual experiences and consciousness create challenges. Emerson said, "The finite wrought and suffer, and the infinite lies in smiling repose. Man thinks of the universe as absolute fact and God thinks of it as liquid law." Many stay in their suffering, rather than allow it to lead them to faith, a deeper knowing and learning of the lessons. People will change the conditions—political parties, churches and relationships—when the solution lies in changing consciousness. In a sense, it isn't even a need to change consciousness, but to awaken to a higher altitude, a higher understanding and greater knowingness. This awakening happens as you come to Spirit, who will guide you as you hear the intuition, which speaks within your heart and soul. The primary objective is to have the God realization. Divine realization in consciousness sets up an energy of life's unfoldment, which allows things to support your direction. When you begin to harmonize with your higher Self, the you who is seeking to be a greater conscious initiative in your world begins to resonate and realize the God consciousness is you. With this realization you are going to feel your body invigorated, and healing is going to happen naturally, not because you're trying to fix a sore arm or a tired back, but because the whole expression is healing.

Remember the first commandment? "You shall put no other God before me." This means you shall not put a problem before God. You shall not put your limitations before God. You shall not put what the doctors say before God. In the comic "Where's Waldo?" Waldo is there in the midst of the crowds. In the midst of our lives, no matter what's going on, God is there somewhere. We put nothing before God; we realize the Presence. It is not by might and it is not by power; it is by a consciousness. When you enter this consciousness your relationships then become dynamic, enriching, revitalizing, insightful and love-filled. Your career is stimulating. You look forward to waking up in the morning and going out to play. This comes from gaining altitude in order to harmonize with the higher aspect of ourselves. When your life is led from this place, your word cannot return void. Heaven and Earth may pass away, but your word will not, until it is fulfilled. This is faith.

It's said the Buddha mind is like a calm, deep, clear lake that reflects the moon of truth, and the ordinary human mind is like a lake that is so churned up with the discontented thought and tumultuous expression that it cannot begin to reflect the moon of truth. Now, where did the moon go? It hasn't moved. It's still there. The body is still there, but it has all the turmoil going on. The clear mind is able to reflect the truth that is there—the presence, the wholeness and the completeness of your being. If your life is not reflecting this kind of connection, it's not as if God has moved or you've lost favor with Spirit; rather, you've allowed the reflection, the connection, to be caught up in the bombardment.

Let us never lose sight that the Source is Spirit, and It shows up through people in different places and circumstances. As we unify ourselves, putting our trust, our faith, our conviction and our assurance in the Divine Power, Essence and Light, it will then begin to unfold because it's all intact. It is all here. As we fly in consciousness into higher states of awareness, to this place of recognition of our oneness with the Power, we'll know as God knows. The answer could be sitting on the other side of the planet, but this doesn't mean you're going to have to go out there and find it. What is essential is to realize God is infinite and It is all right here; you are the very center of this infinite wisdom and life. As you allow yourself to resonate, to fly at this higher altitude, you stop dueling with God and you just are this Power, and It begins to reveal Itself. It begins to make Itself known. It's a matter of the alignment of your consciousness, and the alignment of your thinking within your life.

It's time for us to go beyond appearance, beyond the realm in which we live. It is time for us to gain altitude, moving into a higher place and developing an attitude that is independent of our circumstances, and independent of our present level of seeing and perception.

Life's Daily Gifts

Kabir, the 15th-century Indian mystic poet, said, "When our eyes and ears are open, every leaf on the tree reads like a page of Scripture." Spirit's speaking, waiting to reveal Itself and waiting to impart something wonderful for our soul and our spirit, but we're the ones who have to open up the consciousness and awaken. When you bring this Spiritual consciousness and awareness to the mundane things in life, washing the dishes can become a spiritual experience. Looking out a window you've always looked out, suddenly you can see what is out there in a whole new way. Making a bed can be perceived as actually preparing the bed for God, tucking Spirit into those sheets. You can have these everyday awarenesses if you choose to see Spirit in all things. Everyday experiences can change our being and awaken us to feeling so good inside. Something transpires, elating our soul and quickening our spirit as it opens the eyes, the ears and the being.

If you are flying at this Divine altitude—this place of realization where your heart's feeling good and you know the Presence—there isn't any room for garbage. This principle is true across the sky, so if you're experiencing a challenge in any area of your life, experiencing some lack, limitation, or a challenge in a relationship, go to the place in your heart where you begin to realize, recognize and focus on the presence of God, and there isn't room for the other stuff. When we are looking to gain altitude within our lives, if we can remember to go to the place of the realization of God, joy or fullness of Spirit, there is no room for the other stuff.

The Heart Knows

Russian novelist Fyodor Dostoevsky said, "Only the heart knows how to find what is precious." If you are experiencing something in your life that is less than precious, you don't find what is precious by trying to figure out what is going to make you feel better, but by going to the knowingness. The heart knows what is precious; allow this knowingness to bring you up.

Imagine if you took a part of every hour of every day to think about Spirit. All that other menial nonsense wouldn't be in your experience anymore because the mind, consciousness, thoughts, energy and focus would be on scanning the spiritual horizon. The heart knows this is true! Your heart can soar at this level. Your heart is the authentic compass of your being, which will point in the right direction. It will also tell you if you're heading in the wrong direction; it shows up in your whole being. The heart shows up in your body. Have you noticed that you sometimes just get a sense deep inside that something doesn't quite feel right, or it feels wonderful, or your whole body tenses up, or it relaxes—that it feels the passion inside? This is the whole-being feeling I'm speaking of, and it is how the heart registers its input. As we listen to this spiritual awareness, it doesn't necessarily make rational sense, but there is a knowingness that comes.

There was a Zen patriarch who said, "The great way is not difficult to those who let go of their perspective." If you let go of your precious notions that you're carrying, and begin to open up to what is—God, wisdom, love and abundance—and fly into the place of realization, you are going to experience the wonders of life.

When we are open to the diversity of life, of Spirit expressing, we get surprises in life. When we trust those surprises, we experience new realizations that God is present. You'll shine with the excitement, like Moses after talking to the burning bush—talking to Yahweh!

It's said after Buddha received enlightenment he was walking down the road and a man came up to him and said, "Who are you? Are you a celestial being?" Buddha said, "No, I am not." The man asked, "Well, are you a wizard? Are you a magician?" and Buddha replied, "No, I am not." The man kept asking him, "Are you...?" and he went on. Buddha said, "No, I am not." Finally, the man asked, "Who are you? What are you?" and Buddha said simply, "I am awake." Awake to what? Awake to the presence of God, which is everywhere! Every day, everywhere we can begin to see as God sees and read the Scriptures off the leaves of a tree. The world sings with expression of Spirit. When you start hearing people talk you will no longer see the problem or their fixation or fascination of whatever limitation is keeping them grounded. You will see their Buddha-ness, their Christlikeness, their Godliness or their "higher self-ness," which is already traveling in this higher dimension.

Many people have experienced a lot of disappointment in their lives, so they have come to depend on disappointment, or at least expect it to be consistent in lives. Their hearts have been broken enough times in their lives that they have come to recognize a broken heart as a natural thing. They believe life will go well for only so long and then the good will disappear, dry up and go elsewhere. The brokenhearted tend to substantiate their sense of disappointment because they are working at a subjective level to be able to prepare themselves for the forthcoming difficulties or challenges, so they won't be hurt so badly. This thinking casts a shadow upon one's Spirit of the soul, deadening the joy and well-being. It quiets down the heart, making it more difficult to hear it within our lives. The overcast sky only casts shadows on the ground; the sun is shining already. Spirit is calling for them to take off and move through the thin layer of fog, but they must answer the call by rolling out onto the tarmac.

If we are experiencing pain or difficulty it doesn't do any good just to sit there waiting for God to take it away. You've got to be moving. You've got to take some action on those visions and spiritual truths we so easily espouse. The wonderful thing about reaching out to someone who is lonely, or participating in the love of life, is it feels good. Have you noticed this? When you love, it feels good. Why would you deny yourself such a wonderful and free experience? Imagine if we put a sign out on the road that said "FREE." How many people would show up? There would be a "love in." You don't have to earn it; you don't have to prove you're worthy of love. You showed up here on this planet and you breathe. It's not as if you have to earn air. Your existence is good enough to be a recipient of air and love in your life.

There's an old familiar metaphor that compares us to gold. The gold could be a watch, a chain, a pendant or a cufflink. The truth is that these can all be melted back down into their essence, which is gold. The essence of your being is Spirit. As soon as we begin to lose sight of this, we begin to lose sight of the essence of our being. We begin to forget the higher aspect—our higher self—our Christ consciousness. We forget to fly at those higher altitudes. Ernest Holmes says, "There is a part of us that has never been violated." This is a part of us that has never been violated, and this is the part I'm speaking about here. However, we get caught up in the part of life that feels it's been violated; we become the watch, or worker or spouse, forgetting the essence of our being, which is gold, which is love, which is Spirit and which is pure. Getting caught up in earthly experiences, forgetting our real essence, keeps us flying in the shadows of the obstructed skies.

Think of a gold ring. Can you remove the gold from the ring and still have the ring? Of course you can't! Well, can you extract God from our being and still be? Of course we can't! Right at the very center is Spirit. Right at the very heart of us is God. We cannot remove God, but we can have a sense of separation. With this sense of separation we forget to include Spirit and we become vulnerable to the ways of this world. When we allow this kind of vulnerability we set up situations that stir up turbulence and mess us up emotionally, because we're now flying in this world forgetting the realization of the God presence, which invites us to gain altitude.

God and What?

We all come from God. We come from one Spirit with the freedom of choice, with the infinite possibilities to create. The truth of our nature is infinite potentiality. We have chosen to diversify, to multiply and to experience pieces of the potential. We are all connected to the one Source. When we can remember we can begin to let go of the fears, because those fears have us tethered to the ground.

We must have faith, because with faith our sense of separation is healed. If we begin to see form as ugly or look at a situation as impossible, we are creating a separation. It's essential to know in the midst of all there is love; the Presence is right there. When we slip into thinking there is God and us, this is separation. When we begin to think there is Spirit and form, or Spirit and matter, this is announcing duality. God is in and through all things; there is no separation. With this kind of faith we become a vortex in which the wholeness can once again reveal itself and begin to emerge. So often people begin to think there is God and something else, placing the faith in something outside of themselves. Know we each have direct contact with Source. When we can, as Ernest Holmes says, "…have that faith of God, not in God," then we're not placing it outside. We are the very flight course through which Spirit expresses, and It will express. Gaining altitude we fly into a more harmonious kind of vibration, resonating with the flow and becoming the clear vehicle through which Spirit exposes and expresses Itself.

Let me clarify. What we're dealing with now is not a Power (you know I talk about God being a Power); the creative principle is a Power. The Creator and Its creation is a Power, but what I now speak of is God as a Presence. Within this Presence there is no sin, no lack, no discord, no limitation, no fear, no duality—nothing for a power to overcome. We've gotten into praying to the Power to save us. We've prayed to the Power to bring the supply when we're in a place of lack, like a Western Union delivery: "Father in the sky, please deliver more money." We pray to the Power to heal, but It's not a Power. It is a Presence and when we are able to fly right into the Presence and feel, to unify, to know, to experience, we're going to celebrate because there is no need of a greater power to overcome anything. We'll celebrate our sense of freedom, our sense of fulfillment and our sense of joy. The celebration is about our ability to live the expression of this Presence in all we do without having to fight against anything.

Where Are You Living?

Are you open to those moments of sorrow abating and joy arising in your life? Then remember with greater conviction and clarity your childhood in the Kingdom. Know who you truly are and allow it to come through your whole be-ing—to come through your heart, not just your brain, and come through the whole essence of yourself. When you know this and are guided to the higher altitude, the Christ consciousness, you're no longer in the hangar, but instead living and flying in this world. Yet, you are connected to the Kingdom and the expression of its light in your present location. Your heart knows how to do this. Take a look at some of the greats like Jesus who got insights from meditation and fasting. What did he do afterward? He came out into the world with people. He walked among the sorrowful and hurting, then healing happened. Take a look at Moses up on Mount Sinai. He got great insights, but he didn't stay there; he came down and freed the Hebrews from slavery. Buddha, sitting under his Bodhi tree—BOOM—got it. He didn't stay seated; he got up and walked all of India. Martin Luther King went to the mountaintop and saw the promised land, but didn't stay there. He came back, knowing that when you enter into those higher altitudes it's not about staying there and keeping to oneself. It is about living and sharing the Spirit in all you do, finding time in every hour to remember the presence of God. As you do so, you will begin to discover that you are led on your flight through life by the authentic compass, which is within your being so clearly there is no room for question. You will know, because your heart knows.

In Greece, some monasteries built between the twelfth and the seventeenth centuries were constructed on thousand-foot pinnacles on the cliffs. The monastic way of being was to lower baskets up and down on ropes to bring in the food, people and supplies, because the monks believed the way to Spirit was not to go out and walk among the people, but to separate themselves from the evil of the world by being at a higher place. Correct or incorrect, theirs was a different interpretation of what was right. How many lives did they change by staying in the clouds?

How are you interpreting life? Others may say it's miserable or terrible, but this doesn't have to be your interpretation; it doesn't mean you have to run to a cave and become a hermit. You can choose to walk in this world. I recommend that you begin this spiritual practice with your family, which means as you sit and look across the dinner table, you look and see a saint—Mom and Dad are saints, the children are saints, your spouse is a saint. Begin to look at the presence of God within those individuals. It begins in the home. If you can begin to look in a very loving, saintly, Christlike way upon this individual who definitely knows what hot buttons to push, they can't help but mellow out when they're loved like that. You're the one who gets to choose to practice this principle, to choose to be at this higher level. You'll find something wonderful happens; something shifts inside because of the altitude you've gained.

Ernest Holmes tells us that, "…behind the individual is the Universal, which has no limits. In this concept alone lies the possibility of eternal and endless expansion." Behind the individual is God. Find it all right where you are! It's true for you, it's true for me, and it's true for the drunkard out on the beach and the beggar on the corner. God is always God. This means God is in the person on the street, at the ticket counter, in the relationship, in business, because God is always God and present in all. It's true for the nastiest people in your life; right where they are, God is, the fullness is, and the only thing lacking within their world is a recognition of the Presence, an acknowledgement of the Presence.

Sometimes in our lives we will have discord and we'll be out of balance. Sometimes this discord happens because of a lack of connection. It can happen when we have expectations, thinking what we need is going to come to us from the outside, thinking somebody can take what we have away from us. What is ours is God. Begin to look at the people in your life and in your world and realize they are Spirit. Imagine what it would be like if you looked out at everyone you saw and realized they were your friends. It would feel pretty good, wouldn't it? If everyone out there wanted to assist you, help you and empower you, can you imagine what it would be like to be alive? Every flight course and experience you have is looking for the grace of God to bless you and enrich your world, and it's not because you're trying to make it happen.

Emerson said, "To believe your own thoughts, to believe that which is true for you in your private heart, is true for all. That is genius." These are the voices we hear in solitude, in the heart place I am speaking about. These voices grow faint and inaudible as we begin to focus on the world of effects. Where are you choosing to live?

Sometimes in our lives we get caught up in the karmic stuff —the law of cause and effect. In this physical realm we are dealing with the law of cause and effect, but when we go to the higher altitude, going above and beyond, we stop trying to manipulate the energies, we stop trying to redirect the law and tell God how to do it. Instead we enter into the grace of God, entering an altitude of beauty, which is whole, and where there is warmth, abundance and truth. Get your pilot's briefing from this elevated perspective and allow it to unfold in your world. It is up to us to abide in this level of consciousness, and as we abide within this Presence, we begin to experience the benefits of the grace of God—not because we are telling God what to do, or "mocking up" some vision for God to fill. We experience them because they are the natural benefits of being in this "God place," which is above and beyond our present level of circumstance.

Espousing or Knowing

God is always God, no matter what the emotional storm or the mountain of challenge you might be experiencing in life. No matter what your objective situation may be, remember there is always something hidden in the inner being that has never been violated. We may stall, but the Eternal Voice is forever whispering within our headsets, causing our eternal quest to continue. This is why it is essential to continue to practice Sprit in our life; this is why it is essential to read our Spiritual material and take time to connect with Spirit and Source. It's not just some words, and we're not just praying to our concept of God. We are able to fly into those energy vectors into a higher Spiritual atmosphere.

Jesus talked about the Father; he knew the Father. He knew the Presence and had the experience and a faith that was unshakable. When we talk about Spirit, let us talk from a place of knowingness, not because we are espousing some words we may have heard or read, but because we are resonating with a powerful Energy Force people have sung and spoken about for thousands of years. Have an experience that is beyond words. Become transparent for Spirit; be like a pane of glass letting in the sunlight. How responsible for the sunlight is a pane of glass? The sunlight simply is. Become that transparency. In Philippians it says, "I can do all things…" This is Spirit speaking. When you have that faith, when you believe, you become this "I" in Philippians. When we know God, there is no separation. When we are able to move to this altitude, we are going to find such a power in our lives that all life becomes brighter. The Spirit of God is there, but we have to believe it in our hearts.

Be this transparency for Spirit where you are living life, where you are flying in Spirit, scanning the horizon and recognizing the Presence and feeling a oneness with all life. You are no longer dueling with God; instead there is a sense of unity. It is from this place of recognition and unity with the Source that you are able to realize the spiritual truth in all those pertinent and relative areas of your world. You'll be able to look right at those areas where you could use a little bit more growth without denying they exist. You'll look those spots right in the face and realize the Presence is there. You will begin to know your spirituality by your fruits.

You don't go around feeling spiritual any more than you go around feeling honest. You can be honest and you can be spiritual, and through your actions you can see you're living a spiritual life. If you're thinking or feeling honest, it is usually in comparison to thinking or feeling dishonest; and if there is a sense of dishonesty, there are still remnants inside of the dishonesty in which you are drawing the comparison. In the spiritual life, it's not as though you are feeling spiritual—you are spiritual, I am spiritual. You're one with the Presence and your life will reflect this.

Prayer of Faith

Often we pray, "Hey, God, let me enlighten you to the situation here," or "Let me make a deal with you" (as if I have something God doesn't). God is—that Presence is. When we can have faith in this Presence, we will no longer try to enlighten God. So often we pray in the human mind or the human consciousness. It is time for us to fly into the God consciousness, where health and wholeness are, along with the abundance that lives in the already established "is-ness" of Spirit. Realize it is not you, it is not your power, and it is not about manipulating, coercing or willing from your limited perspective. It is standing in the truth and being all that you are. You've got to have the faith, and when you have faith, it will make you whole.

You are a Spiritual Being! This doesn't mean you are evolving to One, or that you are going to become One; it means you are a Spiritual Being right here and now. It's up to us to have faith and to remember to practice it, allowing the Wholeness to reveal Itself in our lives once again, but we must have this kind of faith and not allow the appearance, the ugliness or anything else to create the separation. There is not God and something else; there is God—period!

Our prayers put our faith back into the power of wholeness and completeness, allowing us to see the part of Spirit that has never been violated—the love energy, the pulsating heart at the center of all. As we work within our own hearts, souls and beings, the Divine picture emerges through the cloudiness and we have the power to move our lives and our world. As we begin to take care of ourselves and our world, the ripple effect occurs and things begin to change. The environment you live in begins to reflect your level of conscious connection.

Teilhard de Chardin talked of the evolution being quantum, meaning it went from no-life to life, from animal life to human life. The growth in our world happens this way. In the next step of evolution, I don't see a singular spiritual leader stepping forth like a great Messiah. Instead, I envision something more like a field in springtime, with the beauty of the flowers popping up—leadership and spirituality will be coming forth from our planet everywhere. The vortex will no longer be just one spot; it will be everyone going out and allowing their deeds to be courageous expressions of God. With belief and trust in the flow of Spirit, you are able to look for the presence of God everywhere. Being connected with Source, you are able to naturally see the Presence and the flow, and you naturally see the gifts of Spirit as wonderful things take place.

From a Distance

As I was sitting on the cliffs, doing my morning meditation and connecting with Spirit, I saw a large pod of dolphins swimming south along the coast. I watched at length as these dolphins demonstrated their individual expressions of dolphinhood. Some were doing flips; others were surfing waves. One baby dolphin kept jumping up and trying to get other dolphins to play. They were doing headstands and nose-stands, and waving their tails. With absolute fascination, I watched the diversity of these dolphins going in different directions, swimming out, swimming back and as I stood up on the cliff I couldn't help but notice that in the diversity of what it was they were doing, there was still a unified flow of southward swimming. They looked extremely diverse, yet from a distant place there was a sense of how they were all moving south together in a cohesive flow. Sometimes we have different people and situations in our lives—maybe we're doing headstands ourselves, trying to hold things together in our world—but we're unable to understand from the individual spot how it is part of the whole picture. If you can gain a little altitude, like sitting on the cliff, and look out upon your life, from this objective distance you will be able to see the flow and the direction of your life—the God flow.

On the spiritual path, it is powerful to be able to gain some distance from activities and diversity, and begin to see how our experiences, our challenges and our joys fit into the flow of our lives. Feel God is there and feel your connection with Spirit, because the truth is, "God is infinite and fills all space." That God is infinite is a basic truth in all religions—and infinite means It fills all space. I've noticed it doesn't seem to have much significance in one's life if one doesn't recognize that the infinite Presence is in their world. If one doesn't have the experience of God through a conscious realization, what good does this statement do them? It's up to you to have this experience, and to allow yourself to unify with this awareness. This is why it is essential to take time in the course of your day to reconnect with your Source and renew your connection with God, so you can understand the unfoldments of your world from the elevated perspective.

Remember what it is like to be with Spirit, and to feel the touch in your life. When I'm talking about God, I'm talking about the Essence, the Life Force—not somebody out there on a throne. I'm talking about the personalized something, which only you can recognize when you feel It. Do you know what it's like when you're having a tough time and somebody just touches your shoulder and says it's okay? All of a sudden you're touched; you feel unified. One touch made you feel okay. It didn't matter what was being said. All of a sudden, somebody touched your shoulder and there was a sense that it was okay. This is the experience we are looking for here—the unification. As we talk about flying with Spirit, it is about unifying, feeling, sensing and knowing. It is about being the flight course of Divine expression.

All these fancy metaphysical concepts are great, but the basic education is the concept of our oneness with God. When we can truly believe in the midst of whatever confusion is in our lives, we can soar above the mountains of challenges with enough clearance to connect with our Source. We'll find that new realms of creativity open up and Spirit reflects amazingly into our world. It doesn't take away from God if we are experiencing It here. Just because I'm experiencing God here doesn't mean

I'm denying your experience of God where you are.

I watched a beautiful full moon reflecting off the ocean, and it didn't take away from the moon at all. The ocean was huge and able to reflect it, and it didn't ruin the ocean. One night I was having dinner late in the evening on my patio. I'd just done some watering, and on my deck there was a little puddle of water. You know what? That big moon was reflecting in the little spot of water on the patio, and it didn't take away from the moon. When the moon shines and simply is, it can light up the ocean or it can light up a little speck of water. It's the light; it is God, and it's not taking away from anywhere or anything. When we can step into the flow, allowing Spirit to have Its way, we will come to discover we're not taking anything away from anyone. We are the bodies through which God reflects, flows and moves.

The present moment is where God expresses; it is where we can feel the unity and it is where this flow is happening. Right here. You do this by gaining altitude, flying into that Christ consciousness and being a channel through which Spirit flows. It moves, It gives and It expresses. It will be far more creative than you could ever be. It will be exciting and dynamic. The truth about you is this: You are greater than any of the stories you could fabricate.

To deepen your awareness and recognition of Spirit, make flight plans in conscious connection with God. Spirit will show you more than you knew even existed. It's up to you to recognize this Presence and allow yourself to begin to unify with It, gaining altitude to enter this higher consciousness. When you get it you have some work ahead of you, because you are a bearer of that Light. For those who have It, much is expected. The light is shining, It is growing; much is expected. But the light shines and healing happens as we gain altitude, entering the glorious atmosphere of Christ consciousness!

COMING IN FOR A LANDING

*While flying through life, there
are times when we reach a destination
(not our final destination, or even our
only destination, but a destination,
nonetheless), and approaching these
destinations with all the cosmic piloting
skills at our command, we come in for a
landing. By this, I mean we bring our
subjective and our physical reality into
alignment. Focusing on the runway
lights of spiritual truth, the Presence and
Allness of God, we maneuver the plane of
our physical reality into alignment with
those lights and watch the manifestations
of our world come into view.*

As I neared my destination one night, the darkness outside
my cockpit window loomed thick and black. Checking
my instruments, I confirmed my location and finally
spotted the runway lights twinkling in the distance. There were
patches of low, wispy clouds drifting below me, blurring visibil-
ity. Further off I could see the lights of the nearby city, but I knew

not to pay attention to them. As dark as it was, I needed to focus on those runway lights. Having reached my destination, I was coming in for a landing. Never losing sight of my goal, I clicked my microphone seven times to turn on the pilot-activated high-intensity lights along the runway. Focusing on the lights at the end of the runway, I didn't allow the other lights to distract me. Night landings require all the skills, knowledge and instincts at my command. I followed all the necessary piloting procedures to bring my plane in for a smooth, safe landing.

While flying through life, there are times when we reach a destination (not our final destination, or even our only destination, but a destination, nonetheless) and approaching these destinations with all the cosmic piloting skills at our command, we come in for a landing. By this, I mean we bring our subjective and our physical reality into alignment. Focusing on the runway lights of spiritual truth, the Presence and Allness of God, we maneuver the plane of our physical reality into alignment with those lights and watch the manifestations of our world come into view.

You may be urged to focus on something other than those runway lights, but coming to the awareness and the belief of God's Presence in the midst of what appears to deny it will guide you safely to your destination. On runways there are lights called VASI (Visual Approach System Indicators) that help one stay on the precise glide slope necessary for a safe landing. Life gives us those indicators if we know how to read them. When we know this, the Divine Power begins to flow easily into our life. Your faith has brought you in for a landing of your choice, for "it is done unto you" at the level in which you believe.

There's a wonderful verse in the Bible that says, "The eyes have not seen, nor the ears heard, nor the heart of man even begun to conceive of the things Spirit has in store for them." We have not even begun to conceive of the things God has in store for us. If we allow ourselves to get locked in, by protecting what we have, or wanting what we don't have, we're putting ourselves in the tie-downs and placing chocks under the wheels of our plane to keep us from our good. Too many are either protecting what they have or wanting what they don't have, just pulling those knots tighter, and we try to free ourselves by using the human mind. Spirit wants to express wonderfully in your world. Lack in your life is the condensation of want. Your wanting is like a dog whistle. When somebody blows it, you don't hear it, but the dogs in the neighborhood come running. You may say, "Well, I'm fine. I'm doing my affirmations. I want this and I want that." It's like blowing the dog whistle on the subjective realm, calling all those dogs into your world—the dogs of challenge taking form in your life as difficulties and scarcity, while you say, "But, I'm doing my affirmations…"

One year Kalli and I were planting palm trees in our garden, and we were amazed by all the different kinds of palms we noticed out there in the world. We noticed the King Palms, the Queen Palms, the Pigmy Palms, the Fan Palms, the Date Palms—all the different palms everybody seems to have around here. The following year we were working on flowers, and suddenly we weren't seeing palms any more—we were seeing all the different types of flowers that can grow in our environment. This is how the mind works. If your mind is focused on how you have been broken in life, you don't see your wholeness. You don't see your well-being or how your life seems to be working. What you're focused on and fascinated with shows up in your world. If you believe there is danger out there in the world, you're focused on fear. What tends to manifest in life is that which supports the level of thought. If we're living with the conviction that "life gets better," we will enjoy our day and at the end of it we will feel it has been a good day. If you were to know life would be over tomorrow, would you still be content with how you spent your time today? To live your life this way—knowing Spirit's presence in the present moment—creates the awakenings of everyday life that make it worthwhile. Sometimes we're still looking in the wrong direction, gazing at the lights of the far-off city instead of focusing on those runway lights when it's time to come in for a landing.

What Are You Looking At?

There's a story the Buddhists share about a man who had gone off to do business. While he was gone a gang of foreign marauders came into his village and destroyed it, burning it to the ground. They kidnapped and killed as many people as they could. When the man returned to his house, it had been burned to the ground and he assumed his young child had been killed as well. He picked up the charred body of a young boy and held a ceremony to honor him. From that day forward he kept the ashes of his young son with him wherever he went—to work, to the marketplace, everywhere. But in reality, when the marauders came into the village they had kidnapped his son and imprisoned him in their village. After many years, his son escaped from his captors. Late one night, the son returned to his father's home. He knocked on the door and his dad, in his sorrow and continual tears, called, "Who's there?" His son answered, "Papa it is me; it is your son." The father, so fixated on his sorrow, said, "It can't be. My son has been killed." The boy said, "But, Papa, it's me. Open the door." His father replied, "You must just be a young boy pulling a prank. Go away!" The kid persisted, knocking and knocking, but the father said, "Go away!" Finally the son stopped knocking and eventually walked away, and father and son were never reunited.

Sometimes we cling so hard to what we believe that we miss out on the gifts in our lives. We put on some beliefs like unbecoming clothing, getting up in the morning and saying, "Well, I'm the one who gets disappointed," or "I'm the one who is disillusioned," or "I'm too vulnerable," or "I'm not the one who gets love in the world." We go out into the world and set it upon the altar of our lives as if it's the absolute truth.

It's time to step beyond this behavior. It's time to have the awakening, the quickening of the soul, which knows you are more than what you've experienced thus far! It's time to let go of last year's style! Sometimes I share this with people and they say, "Well, I'll move when I get pushed…when I get the rules…when I change…when I awaken to a higher state of being…when I get older…when it is my turn…when I get invited…when I get permission…when Santa Claus or miracles show up in life…" Their lists go on and on. Too often we tend to remain fixated on what had once been helpful in navigating to our present location in life, but it's time to accept the handoff from this flight service station to embrace the hand of the next. If we don't accept the new flight watch service, we go forth unprotected or remain in the old air space, closing the possibility of new help. The outside is the unfoldment of our consciousness—our awareness.

Awakening occurs when we realize it does not matter what the world of phenomenon looks like. What matters is keeping the inside focused on the truth and listening to inner guidance. You must believe you can land on the runway of your dreams and take the necessary action to produce the good and positive.

I flew Kalli into Las Vegas for her family reunion. It was the first time I had ever flown into a hectic international airport in my little plane. Generally when I'm flying somewhere and reach my destination, I tend to find the runway and land the plane, which is what a pilot does when he spots his runway. In big international airports, however, they have a different kind of airspace. I had to talk to all sorts of people—clearance control, approach control, deliverance, ground control and the control tower. They were all vectoring me on different paths, so the runway I wanted to land on seemed to be moving farther away from us. They were spacing me out so the big 747s wouldn't come down on top of me or flip me over in the jet wake of their engines. It's crucial to listen to these helpful voices coming over the radio with directions; when they give you a direction, they intend for you to continue on the path until told to do something different. But I wanted to land and they were sending me past the airport, so I started to descend. Apparently I was supposed to maintain a specific altitude (which I think they neglected to tell me). Suddenly I heard a voice over the radio ordering, "Arrow, ascend immediately! Ascend!" Then I heard, "747, descend! Descend!" Well, I got an instant and clear visual in my mind on the possible ramifications of my decision to do things my own way instead of waiting for their directions, so I went up real quick!

Sometimes in our lives we're given insight and guidance and we follow it until all of a sudden the logical mind starts to question: "Did you really mean that? Are you sure you want to do that? Maybe you want to do this instead; it can give you quicker satisfaction." Forgetting the inner guidance we've heard, we no longer listen. We begin to surrender to the discomforts. The discomforts are there to give us the opportunity to correct our flight path, to learn and to grow, and to recognize the lessons directed from inside the cockpit.

"From the inside out" is the way it works. Do you want to hold on to those thoughts and things that make life dark, heavy, nasty and boring, or do you want to have an awakening—one that allows every day to be filled with Spirit, good feelings and exciting times? In order to have this we must take charge of our minds. Remember: You've been given dominion over all things from the skies to the bottom of the ocean. Still, people choose to take this power, this dominion, this word and this ability and use it to fill their minds with limiting thoughts, fear, resentments and materialistic ways. Such a choice is like asking for crumbs when we have been given the Kingdom and the possibility to live in freedom. We have been given the guidance to listen and follow Spirit's lead, yet we've been telling the tower how and where we want to land and, as such, have only been going to God for crumbs.

Start listening and following, and awakenings will happen, bringing richness as the floodgates open into your awareness. You must decide to go to God for God and not for your little things. The Spirit is absolutely talking through the headphones of your consciousness. It's speaking to your being, just waiting to be acknowledged—waiting for your "Roger." Yet we've been like the prodigal son, going out in the world and using up the little we have of our own energy, forgetting it is the Father's good pleasure to give us the Kingdom. This Kingdom has been given no matter what situation you find yourself in life. No matter what it is, Spirit is right there in the midst, but you must accept the direction.

What's Your Interpretation?

Agnostics sit through Sunday morning services and they neither believe nor disbelieve, but they are able to deal with the concept of a life force. Science talks of a life force. We

have Einstein and his theory of relativity. The hermetic philosophy thousands of years ago talked about "…as above so below,
as within so without." A century ago, Edgar theosophists taught
that the mind is the builder of one's reality. Ernest Holmes talked
about the way cause and effect are two sides of thought. Some of
the oldest writings on the planet talk about the one truth, one
energy, which men call by different names. It takes form through
our direction. Thought unfolds itself in our life.

In a survival magazine, there was a story about a guy who
was lost in the desert for days. He was dehydrated, his lips were
parched, his tongue was swollen, his clothes were ripped and his
body was burned from the sun. His legs were cut and bleeding
from crawling through the sand, bugs were eating him and quills
from the cacti were sticking him. As he crawled to the top of a sand
dune, he looked out through his bloodshot, sand-peppered eyes
to the expanse of desert and said, "If this goes on for many more
days, I may become discouraged." What are you going to let get
you? What are you going to let pull you down? What are you going
to allow into your consciousness that's going to ruin your day and
take you to the point that it's no longer fun? Through the alchemy
of your awareness you can allow the mystical, mythical grace of
God to transform your flight through life. You can be looking upon
the same situation from a higher perspective, keeping your focus
on those runway lights of truth, listening to the guidance to get
you out of the old level of cause. If you keep doing the same stuff
in the same way you've been doing it, you won't be landing at new
resorts. Remember the old adage: "If you keep heading in the same
direction that you are headed, it's likely that you will end up where
you are going." You get to land at a grander destination because
the interpretation of God, experience and life lies with you–not the
prophets, seers, sages, mystics or poets. It lies within you.

Out on the banks of a river, a fisherman watched the fisherman next to him with a little curiosity. Every time he would catch a fish, he would put it down next to a ruler. If the fish was bigger than the ruler, the fisherman would throw the fish back. Then he'd catch another fish and put it down next to the ruler, and if it was bigger than the ruler he'd throw it back. After about the third time, the guy watching him was really wondering why the other fisherman was throwing away the big fish, so he asked, "Hey, are you throwing those big fish back because they're too bony, or is it because they don't have enough meat? What's going on?" The second fisherman answered, "Oh, no. My frying pan is only as big as this ruler. If the fish is bigger than the ruler, it doesn't fit into my frying pan."

How big is your frying pan? What size ruler are you carrying around to measure your good in life? Is life offering you good that is too big for your consciousness? Is it too big for your comfort zone? Is there a destination with too much possibility and good for you to come in for a comfortable landing and accept all that is waiting for you in life? Your landing and arrival means feeling the flow empowering you, expanding you beyond your present realm of understanding. It will take you to the very edge and demand for you to be more.

It's important to hold the intent in mind and let go of the how-to's. God, Life, Spirit will give you the how-to's. What's important is the intent. Can you fly in for a landing staying focused on the intent? You're dealing with the infinite Spirit. A lot of times, the subjective—that trickster in your mind, that last, little part of the devil—is going to say you're powerless to change the situation. If you allow yourself to believe you're powerless and imprisoned in this heartless world bouncing out of control, you'll find yourself in absolute chaos, going down in the death spiral. Watch what the mind does. It gets into those beliefs; it gets into the disaster movies and the big challenges in your life and brings them home, allowing them to look so big it concludes, "I cannot have choice in my world," thus giving your power away.

More than Meets the Eye

Have you ever sat down at the dinner table for a family meal? Everything went great; the conversation was good. What was going on there was a lot more than "what was going on there." Have you ever tucked a little child into bed at night? What was going on as you read the child a story? A lot more was going on than "what was going on." This is the inner energy I am attempting to get you to sense. It's not something we get in the head; it's a sense we feel in the heart and whole body. This body of ours is a good vehicle, but we are in a spiritual entity. We are a spiritual being which is using this body; it's our worldly drag, if you will. This worldly drag houses the spiritual entity—the spiritual being that you are. We are standing right at the threshold of a magical moment. All the mystics, the great seers, the sages and the poets tell you the present moment is the home of God. It's the home of love.

This present moment where we reside has the opportunity and the potential to bring forth the fullness of it All, but you're the one who has to get intimate with your spiritual self so you can fly across the threshold runway lights. When you see those lights clearly marking the corridor, you line up and commit to your landing. As you approach and come in for a landing to this wonderful destination on your flight course, you become more fully aware of your true self as heir to the Kingdom. Listen to the direction, become intimate with it so you can find the courage to focus on those lights, fly smoothly through and land. You'll find you're in the land of milk and honey, because the place is one of fullness and abundance. It's love, it's joy and it's happiness. For some mysterious reason, we tend to postpone this—not all the time, but there are some areas of our lives where we have postponed this energy. If this present moment is really the home of God, if this runway is another landing strip to eternity, then it seems to me this moment should be almost the easiest thing to experience. Obviously it's not, because we tend to postpone the fullness of Spirit that is seeking to express Itself. Instead we fail to set our plane down, using up fuel and adding tension.

Have you ever had a time in your life when you were just clicking? You said the perfect thing to the perfect person. Your actions were just so in sync; you were in the flow. Do you know that moment? That's the arrival, the landing I'm trying to get at here. It's always available. What just happened? You connected. You opened up. You trusted. You let go of history or expectation. You brought your plane smoothly down the runway and through the threshold to eternity, where the fullness of Spirit is seeking to express Itself. You've given up the judgment, the history, the expectation.

What keeps us from crossing this threshold, from getting intimate with ourselves and coming to recognize the spirit in which we truly are? We tend to point a finger at what other people are doing and saying, rather than looking inside and recognizing our inner connection and knowing the outside is a message from our inside. What's going on in our world in reality is our consciousness housing itself. Too often we get into analyzing, critiquing and pointing the fingers and we take this infinite power, which we could be working on ourselves with, and put it outside. In order to avoid becoming intimate, we find those people who really bug us and tend to create them in our life. Don't you still have some in your world like that? You are still creating them so it gives you a story to talk about. If you really thought about it, you could eliminate this person's energy from influencing you. See, it's the outside saying, "Hey, look inside here." It's the outside trying to get the message to you on the inside.

People who are out there going from religion to religion, from teacher to teacher in search of...whatever—I find they finally slow down when they come across someone or something that leads them to themselves. Tell those who search to look inside, not to give their power away to some dogmas and some creeds, but to be led by their own inner integrity, by the Spirit inside. When one begins to live in alignment with this flow, this Spirit, then everywhere they look, they'll see Spirit and every day there will be joyful awakenings and connections.

As Emerson said, "Man surrounds himself with the image of himself." We surround ourselves with the image of ourselves. Do you want to know where your mind is? Look at your life. Life is a reflection of who you are. What do you say yes to in your world?

Crack the Whip and Speak

There was an animal trainer with the Barnum & Bailey Circus, who was doing a night show. Just as he stepped into the lion and tiger cage and locked the door behind him there was a power outage. All the lights in the Big Top went out, and the crowd said, "Ooohhh!" Lions and tigers are able to see just fine in the dark, and this trainer was at quite a disadvantage. While most of the crowd was unaware of this, the people who worked at the circus were very aware of this and feared for the trainer's life. A few minutes later when the lights came on, there was the trainer, standing in the cage fully composed. He hadn't been eaten or attacked. Afterward, when he was interviewed by the media, they said, "Everyone knows cats are able to see in the dark. What was it you did that enabled you to live through the experience?" He answered, "Yes, the cats are able to see in the dark, but they don't know I can't." He had stood in the cage, giving commands and cracking his whip. This illustrates how important it is for us, when we are in the dark and when things seem tough, that we are able to step into what we know and crack the whip and speak those words to assist us to move to a place until the lights come on, until we are once again in alignment with Source. When the lights go out and the healing that is necessary in your life does not appear to be present, stand your ground, crack the whip and believe.

Of course we love God! Of course we love this "spiritual stuff"! Of course we love…! But can you bring it down to earth and practice it in your life? Can you really have the experience and the activity of God as your consciousness, as your life? When you are in the most precarious of times and things seem dark, are you able to fly forth from this place in mind? Rather than being grounded, slipping into a place of inertia or dullness, are you able to fire up the engines? Are you able to go through the procedures to fly out of this consciousness of apathy, doubt or fear?

Can you take the time to discipline your mind, your being and your life, in order to connect continuously with your Source? This means waking up and saying thank you to God, finding the time—a half-hour or an hour within your day—to connect with Spirit. I'm saying an hour in your day, but it should be every hour of your day to remember and experience the Presence. People say, "But, Christian, I'm so busy. How can I find an hour within my day?" Is Christ realization worth getting up a half-hour earlier?

Is It worth staying up a half-hour later? If your day is so packed that you have 12 hours just absolutely jammed, what's with the other 12 hours? It's your choice. I can't tell you that you have to do it. It is something you must make a priority within your life if you want to feel your Oneness with Spirit, if you want to walk in Spirit and continuously know your Source. It is a conscious discipline. As I'm flying and my mind is on where I'm going, I'm constantly monitoring my instruments to make sure all those necessary to support my flight are still working. Are you constantly monitoring your connection with Spirit?

I read a story about a ranger at Yellowstone Park, who was taking tourists around to see the sights. As they walked up to a bluff where he was showing them the flowers and the wildlife, his radio kept chattering and talking and he got tired of listening to it, so he turned it off. He went on to point out and explain the wildlife in the park. A little while later, another ranger came huffing and puffing to the place where they stood and said, "Why did you turn off your radio? We've been trying to contact you for the last half-hour. There is a grizzly bear stalking your tour group."

Often when God is speaking, when the lessons of life are speaking and the love of Spirit is talking to us, we turn off the walkie-talkie. Turning off the speaker, we say, "I'm not paying attention. God will provide. Everything's going to be okay, so I'm not going to take a look at the fact that life is talking to me. I'll be taken care of; after all, God is love." We don't pay attention. How loud does Spirit have to speak? How much pain is enough pain before we say, "Enough is enough"? You have the power, because the power is God. The Power is looking for expression and it is looking for expression through you! Rather than experiencing the Divine Source, and the connection, and the passion, and the fire that comes from the soul, too often we turn off the radios.

Some people will go from relationship to relationship, loving the excitement of turbulence. They're the drama queens or kings who absolutely love drama and turmoil in their life, so when it calms down they move on to the next near-fatal landing. It's the same pattern emerging—they get caught up in what appears to be a wonderful, new taste and then, all of a sudden, it just becomes bland. They become enchanted with a new face, and soon it becomes common; their visions start out exciting and soon become ordinary. This is what happens when one is living from outside stimulus.

In the spontaneity of your willingness to let go to God, to let go to love and to the unfoldment of life as your experience, you will find things don't just happen accidentally. Nothing spiritual is by accident. You'll discover patterns, which you may be unaware of, unfolding as your life. These patterns showing up in your world reflect where you might be falling short and where you've got your act together. You will find that you're so much worthier than you ever realized. Life is seeking to support you, to love you in ever greater ways than your little mind can grasp. As you are willing to step into and practice this, you will be empowered. Ernest Holmes wrote:

> *Suppose we find ourselves impoverished. We wish to change the condition. We know that it is not in accord with the Ultimate Reality; that Spirit imposes no limitations. Therefore, we know that our apparent limited condition has no real law to support it; it is simply an experience of consciousness. We wish a definite result in the opposite direction. First, we realize that the Law of Life is a Law of Liberty, or Freedom. We now state that this Law of Liberty is flowing through us and into all our affairs. But the image of our limitation persists. Here is a definite contradiction*

of our statements of freedom. Right here, we must stop and de-
clare that these images of limitation are neither person, place nor
thing; that they have no power, personality nor presence and no
real law to support them.

Does this happen to you? You say these spiritual words and
your life still looks decidedly unspiritual? Right here, Ernest says,
we must stop. When we say these words and our world doesn't
change, we must begin to fill our thoughts with the ideas of
faith, the expectation of good and the realization of plenty. We
must sense and mentally see right action in our lives. We put our
whole trust in the Law of Good, and It becomes very real to us
as we definitely speak it into our being. Stop and look challenge
in the face. Often people run around and deny they're coughing
and say they're not coughing, when some loud, obnoxious sound
is coming from their throats. Stop and look at it—acknowledge
you're not physically well. But know there is no real essence of
life to support this state. It is up to you to keep the body sick or
well. You can say, "Hey, it's sick, and you know what, the spiritual
truth of this situation is one of wholeness; the spiritual truth of
this situation is completeness, the spiritual truth of this situation
is health." When something is out of kilter in your life, it is a sign
to you—a biofeedback system that something is out of balance on
the inside. Things don't just happen—they happen justly. Listen
to the signs life speaks to you, because if you don't, life's going to
holler them to you louder. Some time ago, I was driving in Carm-
el Valley through an area where it gets flooded from time to time,
and there was a sign that said, "Road Flooded; Do Not Enter;
Road Closed." I looked down the road and I didn't see any flood.
"It must have dried up by now," I figured, and I drove down the
road. A few blocks down I made a turn, drove a little bit farther

and, sure enough, there was a big lake right across the road. With no way to go across it, I drove back and on the other side of the sign that had told me not to go down the road, I read, "Welcome back, dummy."

Life is speaking to us all the time, but are we paying attention? Are you reading the signs that are there? Are you trying to impose your way and trying to say what is right and what is wrong to the great traffic controller in the sky? It is up to us to believe in our higher selves. A lot of times the reason the healing doesn't happen in our lives, or there's a lack in our healing process, is because we are looking for a specific healing of a situation. In a sense, this is right, but it's a missed approach because there is a sense of sickness, or there is a sense of lack or a sense of unwell-being. What we want God to do is to fix a particular situation because we are saying, "This is what I think is right here." This is our little mind focused on trying to fix something. This isn't how we use the Power. We use the truth and Power of God when we allow It to use us. We use it by going to God and working on embracing the Wholeness, the Completeness. This eliminates that which does not belong in our experience, because there is no room for anything unlike it. We don't need to tell God how to correct the situation; Spirit will tell us how to correct it. It will give us the vectors to fly in for our perfect landing. This may look like going to a doctor for antibiotics, or it may look like going to an herb shop, or it may look like just sitting out on the cliff and communing with nature. The key here is going to Spirit to experience our Completeness and our Wholeness, not trying to take our human perspective and say, "God, this is the way it should be."

I was doing an Ordination in Hemet and I thought it would be fun to fly Kalli out to Palm Springs for lunch first, then fly over to Hemet in the afternoon, returning home that night. We just happened to be between two storms, so I called the weather service in the morning and asked, "The clouds look like they're breaking. Can I make it?" They answered, "No, we don't recommend it." It started to clear up later in the day, right around lunchtime. The skies were blue, so I called and they said, "Going over the pass into Palm Springs there is convectional activity, which is what creates the thunderstorms and the big clouds. We do not recommend it. When you fly into Hemet it's going to be very milky. It could turn to fog anytime. By the time you get back in the evening, the fog will be a marine layer, making it difficult to see the ground, so we don't recommend flying." As it got to be late afternoon, I thought I'd call one more time and they just said, "NO!" I looked and the sky was clear. I looked out at the passes, and I knew I could make it. Then I remembered the flood sign. Why am I thinking, if I'm not going to listen? Finally I decided to drive instead. As we did so, the skies remained seemingly clear enough to fly. When we got back home, the fog wasn't too thick and again I thought for sure I could have landed the plane. Once again I began to question the advice of the weather service, thinking, "Maybe I should never listen to them again," when it suddenly dawned on me—if Spirit has spoken, one doesn't need to question. One needs to listen!

You may not know the real reason for something, but if you were attached to a particular answer for a particular purpose and there was a full spectrum of other energy at play, you would not begin to know. Maybe I would have crashed. Who knows what could have been? (I choose not to cross that threshold in my thinking.) If I try to fit it into my own parameter, I'm coming from such a small, inductive place. Spirit sees deductively. Spirit sees the whole. Let's remember to go to God, calling forth the Presence in our lives. When It speaks, let's read the signs it places before us and listen to what comes forth. Let's know we don't have to second-guess, because we believe and trust the direction in which we are guided is for our best and highest good.

Do you know there is a lot of growth going on in your life and your world? Choose to get those lessons life is sending your way! Stop turning off the radio and listen. Get out there and do it. Stop saying, "Oh yeah, God will take care of it." Break the inertia and start your engines. It's time to take flight. When you approach those life destinations, focus on those runway lights of spiritual truth, listen to the Divine direction from within and come in for a smooth landing to a great reality in your world!

CHAPTER ELEVEN

190

FLYING WITHOUT A PLANE—
IMMORTALITY

What you discover is that God is in
you, Spirit is in you. Pain or challenges
make you go down, dig deeper in order to
lift you to a higher state so you can soar.
They assist you to evolve above the
journey of your past, which has also been
wonderful, glorious and challenging, but
whose purpose has been served.

I had the opportunity to stretch myself—I went skydiving for the first time with a couple of friends from Seaside Church. We went to a place called Nicholas Field, which is actually just a stretch of dirt called a runway nestled between some mountains along the Mexican border, next to a lake. Before you begin the course, they have you sign a contract; the following is just a small excerpt from the first page:

Here are the unavoidable facts of skydiving life: Our staff is comprised of human beings who can make mistakes that can result in your injury. Your equipment has been designed by human beings, and it is not perfect. It can malfunction. Your training can never be totally adequate, because there is no physical way to simulate a free-fall while remaining on the ground, the only way to simulate it is to do it, and then it is too late to see if you can perform satisfactorily. Jumping out of an airplane is a very dangerous thing to do. Please don't ever say that we told you skydiving was safe. It is not. While we work very hard to minimize the risk of skydiving, by its very nature sky diving is inherently dangerous and will never be totally safe. We do not guarantee that your parachutes will operate properly. We do not guarantee that our staff will function without error. We do not guarantee that you will land in the right field. We do not guarantee that our backup devices will work correctly. But most of all, we absolutely do not guarantee that you won't get hurt or killed skydiving, even if you do everything you were trained to do. The human body is not designed for the downward landing impact, and it may break. Typical skydiving injuries consist of broken legs, ankles, wrists, fingers, back injuries, injuries of all sorts, including death from hitting obstacles such as power lines, trees, roadways or water, and death from hitting the ground too hard, including airplane crashes.

I wonder if we agree to a contract like this before coming here to Earth? It sounds a lot like life. After reading this contract I was looking for some words of assurance, and realized there's no comfort when you decide to jump out of a perfectly good plane! One of the friends I was jumping with is an attorney; having never seen a contract quite like this one before, his head was spinning, but we went ahead with our plans.

That morning they put us through exercises on how to pull our parachutes in case there's an emergency, and how to land. While still on the ground I attempted to get the "how to" repetition in my awareness, so when I was up there and confronted with…I didn't know what…I could function—keeping my mind thinking. When you jump out of a plane from our altitude, if you don't pull your parachute, you have 20 seconds from the time you leave the door before you meet the ground and inherit the earth, so you have to keep your brain functioning at all times. It's a very fast sport!

Let me tell you, when you're up there with your heart pumping and they open up the airplane door with more than 100-mile-an-hour winds blowing through and hitting your face, and you look out and see the ground moving thousands of feet below, you can't help but wonder, "What am I doing here?" At that moment, my head began to make a lot of sense when it said, "Human beings weren't made to jump out of airplanes at high altitudes. What is it you are really going to get out of this experience?" Yet there was something inside of me that wanted to go. What was I going to listen to? At this point one still can say, "I went far enough, I met my fear, I had enough," or you can step out. Once out the door, however, it is no longer safe to turn back.

There is a quickening of the soul when the jump master says, "Go!" It is an amazing experience to step out of a moving airplane way above the ground. I held on to the strut under the wing with my hands, my feet flapping behind my ears like a flag in the wind. One knows they have to go, but there's a part of you which wants to hold on until the plane lands. As I let go, I had five seconds for my parachute to open up, and you're supposed to count,

"One thousand, two thousand, three thousand…" I was counting, "One God, two God, three God, four God…" Five seconds has never been so long in my life! One can absolutely experience time standing still. I saw lifetimes go before me; I thought about the most intricate things that this planet knows within the five seconds that I waited for my parachute to open. I clearly watched the plane fly away as I literally flew through the air, and when the parachute opened it was such a comforting feeling! I breathed, "Thank you, God." Floating down was peaceful and harmonious. I landed perfectly in the right field. In the moment when it was time to pull my parachute open, I had already dealt with the fear and I knew I was going to be fine. As I was falling through the sky, I realized I didn't know the exact particulars for which to be praying, but I did remember to go to God—to speak the name of God and turn to Spirit, to the Higher Power. Those five seconds waiting for the parachute to open seemed like an eternity, yet I had my mind turned to Spirit, not the fears.

The harmony and peace I found as I met this whole new experience came because I was able to turn to God and know the Presence in the midst of confusion. It is this same turning to God and knowing the Presence that brings untold peace and harmony in facing the ultimate change in flight pattern—that of letting go of the body, surrendering to Spirit and flying without a plane.

What's Beyond?

We have been on a wonderful journey in life, a flight that has taken us through all sorts of enchantment, wonder and joy, playfulness, pain, sorrow, turbulence, forgiveness, ecstasy and bliss. It's been about the mind showing up in physical form, and we have gone right to the very edge, which is the portal to beyond. Yet, there is something beyond what you consciously know. We've flown this whole journey, and you know what? There's another journey out there waiting for you—a journey you fly without the plane of your physical form. All this work you have done has gotten you ready for this very moment—the moment in which you are at the threshold, the portal to something that is beyond, which is incredible. I don't want to just be reporting to you what's beyond. I hope and trust you are encouraged, enticed and excited about discovering what is there after jumping out the door.

What's beyond where you are right now in your life? Are you willing to let go and fly across the threshold? Are you willing to die to the old? When people hear the subject of death, they say, "Oh, death, that's so morbid. Don't talk about death. Talk about transformation. Talk about resurrection. Talk about the phoenix coming out of the ashes, but don't talk about death." There are so many taboos around this subject. It's time to embrace the "D-word." It's a wonderful metaphor, used from the very beginning of time.

Since the first human being contemplated his first breath, there has been ritual around this concept of death and transition. They have discovered the graves of Neanderthals in Turkey, which are 100,000 years old. These graves indicate the Neanderthals performed rituals in the way they took care of those who died or let go of their physical bodies, proving even 100,000 years ago in the primitive state of self-awareness that there was a belief in more than what is here. The Neanderthals are not alone in this belief; Plato wrote about his great teacher, Socrates, in his *Apology*. In this work, Socrates speaks:

> *You too, gentlemen of the jury, must look forward to death with confidence and fix your mind on this one belief, which is certain,*

that nothing can harm a good man either in life or after death.
And his fortunes are not a matter of indifference to the gods, for
the present experience of mind does not come about accidentally.
I am quite clear that the time has come when it is better for me
to die and be released from my distractions.

If he hadn't died the way he did, he would be just another philosopher in history. However, because he was willing to drink the
hemlock and be a martyr, we now remember him. If Jesus had not
died the way he did, he may have been just another preacher in
the hills of Galilee. We may never have heard his message. We had
to see the wisdom and consciousness of these individual triumphs
over our greatest fear, which has been death. At the end of one
state of awareness, one comes to the threshold and the initiation
is offered by the opportunity to meet one's fears. Are you able to
step out of this plane, or do you resist until the vehicle can no
longer fly and you have no choice?

Good Package

The Tibetan Book of the Dead talks about getting the body ready and how to make the journey from here to
there. The Egyptian Book of the Dead talks about the crossing
over and how to do it. Both books are very heavy, and speak of
the strongest power in either dimension. Both talk about Love,
the God power, the spiritual power and the Force that is waiting
for you beyond. The Talmud, a wonderful Jewish text, spiritual
in its depth, says that no atoms in the whole vastness of the Universe have ever been lost. How could we think the soul of man
could be lost? It can't be. We are the ones who have to be willing
to step through that portal, let go of the wing of the plane that

we cling to, and be willing to die to the old form, but we have grown very accustomed to who we are. We like our package. I know mine works for me. What we have is an ego, or our vanity, or our biography. We've got "who I am," and "what I have done," and "this is my history," and it locks us into time and space. With being locked in comes thoughts such as: "Oh, I can't die. This is scary stuff. I'm going to lose all I've worked for." This vanity and self-absorption is the greatest illusion that has grasped our minds. The great teachers all say, "Let go! Trust in the immortality, in the continuity of the soul."

We learned at a very early age to like the biography, or the attention. Look at little babies; they're masters at getting attention. They have learned all the tricks of the trade: sad-eyed pouts, tantrums and looking cute. They're little people who know how to just look at you so you "goo-goo" and make funny faces. You'd never do that for an adult. As we mature, we become more discreet in our attention-getting tactics, but advertisers know the importance of getting our attention.

Advertisers know there is a part of us that still wants to be noticed. They know how to go right for your emotions, right to what matters. I got a letter the other day from an advertiser trying to sell me a periodical. The letter read, "Dear Rev. Sorensen: Our research indicates you are a very intelligent, highly esteemed, well-read man, on the cutting edge of progress. Our research also indicates that you enjoy science and New Age material..." I needed to read no further. Smiling in modest satisfaction, I thought, "Why, it's uncanny—they know me perfectly!" and I subscribed.

This is the tomb we get locked in. The stone gets rolled in place and this vanity, this biography, this identity, which looks like the plane, keeps the door shut as it runs out of fuel. There's no way we're going to step through the portal and merge with the

One and experience the ecstasy if we're locked in. It is time for us to roll the stone away from the tomb, jump out of the plane and soar toward the light.

It sounds simple, but you know what? We like what we have created, and it is tough. This is why we find stories of the sacred wound in so much Western literature. The wound inflicted severs one's whole being, rocking the foundation upon which one stands. Achilles' heel, Orpheus's decapitation, Zeus's split head or Persephone's rape—the list goes on through all cultures. When there is a sense of pain or loss, something cracks, allowing the light in. It opens up the flesh and soul, filling our present state of being with something beyond our ordinary boundaries of knowledge—beyond what we know. When we experience the sacred wound in our lives, we tend to reach for something more than what we have known in the past in order to get us through. We then begin to search for the larger picture, the larger story, the larger meaning of our life. This kind of searching is what allows us to rise triumphantly above the world of form, but something has to have opened us to this. Something has to have penetrated our comfortable, fixed state, so we are fee to jump, to let go of the wing of the plane and soar beyond the known.

You have flown this journey, which has been filled with wonder and been spectacular, but there is more waiting for you. It is exciting! But you have to allow the story of who you are stay back in this world. On this new journey there is a new flight plan for you. Being part of this is wonderful, but you've go to be willing to let go.

Often as people experience the sacred wound they try to cover it up, or they go to a counselor and talk about everything but the wound, carefully talking their way around it. Good spiritual counselors help you take the bandage off the wound. They create a place that may not even feel safe and may even feel disruptive, but that allows you to stir in the pain and the confusion of now knowing so you dig deeper down inside of yourself, and discover what is in you. What you discover is that God is in you. Spirit is in you. Pain or challenge makes you go down and dig deeper in order to lift you to a higher state so you can soar. They assist you to evolve beyond the journey of your past, which has also been wonderful, glorious and challenging, but whose purpose has been served.

Part of the Whole

I had lost a friend who had made his transition, and I was sitting out on the cliffs in front of my house, meditating. It was one of those mornings when the sun was arriving in the east, and the moon was still hanging out over the ocean with its big, long glow across the blue, rippling water. Looking into the sun, all of a sudden, it hit me—my friend was being absorbed into that flame, into the glow, he was going back into the light. Within the light he still had his individual flame, but he was still part of the one bright light—and the bright light was touching me in this moment. I could feel the presence and know there was connection with this unity. He had gone beyond this temporal world, this world the carnal mind knows, into something greater. A peace filled me. Looking at the moon setting down below the ocean, it dawned on me that the moon was not being destroyed; it was not disappearing for good. It was as full, complete and ever-orbiting as when it hung in the sky before my eyes—it only left my sight. The shift took place, which is how we cross the threshold.

Pushed or Pulled

This journey you have been on has been preparing you, fueling you with the strength and the courage to move forward. We have been dealing with the mind, and the body, and our physical world. Are you able to move beyond form, allowing Spirit to soar creatively through you? It takes a knowingness and desire, but that desire in you will assist you in accomplishing what your heart yearns to do, what your soul cries out for, knowing you are capable.

A ten-year-old boy was failing math. He just never got any of the answers right. His parents helped him with his homework and hired a tutor for him. They tried everything but he continued to fail math. Finally his dad said, "That's it! Off to parochial school for you," and off he went. The first day after class, he came home and walked right by his mom. He sat down in his room and feverishly started working, spreading his books all over the place. Stopping for dinner, he gobbled down every last thing on his plate just like a young boy would do, and then went back to his room, closed his door and continued to work for a couple more hours. This practice went on every day; it became his routine. Finally the first-quarter report card came out. The little boy came home with his report card, but didn't say anything to his Mom and Dad. He just set it down on the dining room table and went into his room. His parents opened up the envelope and pulled out the report card. To their astonishment, under math was a big, red "A." They were filled with joy, "This is great!" they said. They went into their son's room and asked, "Hey, was it the nuns who helped you?" The boy answered, "No, it wasn't the nuns." They asked, "Well, was it the tutoring?" He shook his head. They asked, "Was it the peer mentoring?" He said it wasn't. They asked, "Was it the text book, new curriculum?" He replied, "No, no, no it wasn't any of those, Dad and Mom." Curious, his dad asked, "What was it?"

"Well," the boy answered, "the first day when I went to school and I walked in that door and saw that man nailed up there on the plus sign, I knew they were serious!"

This story illustrates a wonderful, universal sign perceived in an interesting way, but how long do you think the philosophy using fear is going to assist somebody once they step beyond that which is known? Fear may push you for a while, but it does not give you the tools to operate in the realm beyond. It is love, joy, integrity, honesty—these are the spiritual qualities that continue with you. For so long, people have been pushed forward on their journey, through fear, through manipulation and control. It is time to let it go! Be pulled by the glory.

Kabir, that wonderful Eastern mystic, wrote many years ago:

> *If you don't break the ropes while you are alive, do you think ghosts will do it after? The idea the soul will join with the ecstatic just because the body is rotten, that's all fantasy. What is found now, is found then. If you find nothing now, you will simply end up with an apartment in the City of the Dead. If you make love with the Divine now, in the next realm of awareness you will have the face of satisfied desire.*

Are you making love with the Divine now? Is your face one of satisfied desire? If Spirit is everywhere present, it is as fully available here as It is there. The New Age concept of dying and finding peace, tranquility and going home is the modern version of the gold-paved streets and harp-playing angels. If God is truly Omnipresent, you are not going to find Spirit any more somewhere else than you can right here.

Who you are is not a mixture of chemicals. You're not a bag of bones. Who you are is animating this bag of bones, this mixture of chemicals. You are an energy; as the Talmud says, you cannot disappear, you cannot go away. Science has proven this by demonstrating that energy can enter and leave space-time. In quantum physics one can see something here and then it's gone, and then it shows up somewhere else—but they don't know how it gets there. Fascinating stuff! To my questioning mind it says, "So, what's beyond this space-time? What's out there beyond—in the gap?" You're the one who has to cross the threshold to know through experience. You're the one who has to go there to know.

Nothing can keep us from stepping into the continuum of life. You are immortal now, yet the understanding doesn't fit it into our earthly package. It doesn't fit into our five—maybe six—senses. When we allow ourselves to be bound only to these senses, it keeps us from jumping into a greater stage of understanding and a greater expression of awareness. What we know is not absolute reality. What we know is relative reality. Our reality is what is relative to us, here and now. It's time for us to go outside of the sense.

The residents of an underground city were quite adjusted to their life underground. In fact, many of them had never even ventured out of their city to the land that was said to be above ground. One day a couple who lived in this city happened to meet a traveler who was visiting from this land above ground. From time to time, visitors came and spoke of that land filled with sunlight, stars, oceans and greenery, but this couple had always taken the tales they'd heard secondhand as boastful exaggerations. However, they happened to befriend this particular traveler, and they invited him to be a guest in their home. During the time he spent with them, he grew homesick and nostalgic and often spoke of his home above ground. Seeing the woman pruning her mushrooms, he said, "Ah, where I come from we have roses that grow in the most beautiful array of colors. Their fragrance, well, it's so sweet, so pleasing, it can't be described by words." Later, watching the man view the city lights upon coming home after a day at work, the visitor sighed and said, "Where I come from we have sunsets, where the sun, a fiery orb of fuchsia light, sinks behind the horizon and the sky is alive with opal-colored streaks—orange, red, pink, lavender—every shade you can imagine!" Soon their visitor grew so homesick that he thanked his hosts for all their hospitality and set off to return home.

In the days following his departure, the couple grew more and more intrigued about this land their visitor had spoken of with such love and longing. Perhaps all the tales hadn't been exaggerations. "I'd like to smell a rose," the woman said. "And I'd like to watch a sunset," the man replied. They decided to take a trip above ground and they were met with thick, gray clouds blanketing the sky. The first plant they came upon was a cactus. "That must be a rose!" the woman exclaimed, and she rushed over to the small bloom of a cactus apple on it and stooped to smell it. The prickly thorns hit her nose and she smelled absolutely nothing. "Sweet fragrance, ha!" she scoffed, gingerly plucking the thorns from the tip of her nose. The sky continued to fill with clouds, growing darker and darker, and a driving wind whipped up all around them. They waited for the beautiful sunset their visitor had spoken of, only to be pelted by the wind-driven sand. Finally the man spat, "Sunsets—bah!" Touching her sore nose, his wife looked at him and declared, "I don't care for roses, and sunsets don't appeal to me. Let's go home." He agreed wholeheartedly and they hurried home to their underground city.

Can you imagine somebody saying that? "I don't care for roses, and sunsets don't appeal to me." This is exactly what we're saying to the other aspects of Spirit, which are calling us forward to experience Its full expression in life. You are the one who gets to say "Yes!" to it. You are the one! Most people who believe that when one dies, death is it—the end—and they find it a scary thought! In the meantime, though, they're living life and they're miserable. They're struggling, so they've got nothing now and their flight and their journey through life is to nothing. Could you imagine living in nothing and going to nothing?

Those of an expanding consciousness, of a Christ consciousness, are aware that there is more than meets the eye. (We're dealing with metaphysics: "meta" meaning beyond, and "physics" meaning the physical.) With this consciousness we know there is more, giving us comfort to step out of the plane, let go of the known and trust the spiritual process. The Divine then becomes the activity of your life, making every moment a scared moment—making every thing, every person, every situation a divine situation. Begin to recognize the very presence of God showing up. Those living in a sense of fear of the unknown keep themselves strapped into the plane of time-space. They don't know what is beyond the time-space thing, so they remain stuck. There is more to you than meets your body.

While working on the first *Catch the Spirit* book, my flight instructor, Tom, was going through some painful family losses. Tom is a rugged former marine sergeant who served in Vietnam, but for all that's tough about him, Tom actually has a heart of gold. Over a period of several months, his son Michael was experiencing some extreme weight loss due to a parasite that had found its way into his body. To the ultimate devastation of Tom and his wife, Michael passed on.

At the time of his passing, Michael's mom saw him in his cowboy boots and new leather coat with fringe, stepping into a bright light with arms coming forth to hug him. This vision brought her some comfort.

When they were inviting people to the service, they attempted to contact Michael's very favorite caregiver, an African-American woman. This caregiver was special to Michael and had helped him overcome a prejudice he'd acquired after being knifed by another African-American. Amazingly, Michael's favorite caregiver couldn't be found. When Tom and his wife contacted the agency that had sent her, the agency claimed they had never known her.

Shortly after Michael died, his wife became extremely ill. A friend who was watching over her at home said she saw someone with a leather coat walk into the other room, so she got up to see who was there—and there was no one. Upon her return to the room, the friend discovered Michael's wife had passed.

The following month, Tom's dad was having an operation. The surgery had been successful and his father was in recovery when Tom received a call to race back to Colorado because his dad had suddenly lapsed into such a state that the doctors didn't expect him to live for 24 hours. Tom hopped on the first plane back to Colorado and was greeted at the airport by his niece. He was surprised to see her, since he hadn't seen her since she was a little girl. She told him that earlier in the day, when she was putting on her makeup, Tom's dad seemed to appear to her in the mirror. He beckoned her to come close because he had a message he wanted her to deliver to his wife.

When they got to the hospital, Tom's niece shared the things his dad had given her to say. They were things only Tom's dad and his wife would have known, including his pet name from their courting days, which no one else had ever heard. Included in the message was Tom's father's request for forgiveness. As the family circled the bed during his final breaths, Tom's niece saw a young man step from the outside of the circle wearing cowboy boots and a fringed leather coat and take the old man's hand. When she described the young man, she described Michael, whom she had not seen since their childhood.

Upon their return home, Tom and his wife found a package on their front porch, which was strange since nothing is left on front porches in this particular neighborhood. However, no neighbors had seen it delivered. When they opened the package, it was a framed picture of the vision Tom's wife had seen before her son's death, arms coming out of a light to embrace a young man stepping into it.

Some might try to explain away each and every one of these incidents; some might even remain convinced that nothing beyond the physical was going on, and still others might say Tom's whole story was nothing more than a series of coincidences. Yet the events cannot be explained away with any degree of satisfaction—certainly not to Tom and his wife. Tom's is just one of countless stories demonstrating the mystical miracle surrounding death, and showing there is more to us than meets this physical body.

People have talked about phantom limbs—limbs they have lost but continue to feel present. In 1935 at Yale Medical School, Dr. Saxton Burke described the electrical-magnetic field surrounding the human body. This isn't anything new. Practicing Kirlian photography, researchers have taken a leaf, torn it in half and put it under a camera, and found that the photo reveals the full figure of the leaf. (They call it the phantom leaf picture.) The energy is there; it is not bound to a body. The body surrounds and expresses the consciousness that you are, so it's up to you to embrace a higher consciousness—to allow yourself to be so impregnated by Spirit you can feel and know and love It. Allow yourself to go beyond.

Rumi talked about death as being the wedding day with the infinite. The Sufis talk about it as the consummation of one with their beloved. Allow yourself to be filled with this Spirit. Allow yourself to know this end is just a beginning. At this point in your life you have come to a threshold, which opens up to an infinite expanse with a vista grander than you could ever have imagined, but you're the one who must fly through it. You must fly into that place. Words only allude to the experiences we have or we know, and words cannot describe what I'm attempting to have you feel.

Buddhists see life and death as one whole: Death is the beginning of another chapter of life; it is a mirror in which the entire meaning of life is unfolded. As the whole meaning of life unfolds the "I" that is looking out cannot be dying. If the "I" believes in dying it is the "I" that is the dying, and the "I" that is looking at the dying. The "I" looking out at the eternal knows the continuity of life. It begins to be absorbed into the recognition of the whole; it is the eternal looking at the eternal. It is the entry into the mystical awareness that lifts you to a whole new state of being. As you're lifted to this new state of being, flying over the threshold to something beyond, you will awaken every aspect as your being begins soaring in a way you have never known. Your whole essence, your whole energy is soaring in a way that is beyond the words. The "I" known as the "I am" is the twinkle in your eyes. While the "I" has lost sight of the truth of its divine and eternal nature, the "I am" that is in your heart is the "I" that knows the infinite, which is God proclaiming Itself as you. It is this knowledge that shatters the reason of the "I" against the doors and walls of truth. There is the theophany of Spirit. You are taken to your very edge of exhaustion, anger, love, pain, sorrow and bliss, so your whole being cracks, allowing the light to enter. This part in you free-falls from its present mode of transportation and is liberated. It is your soul feeling the ecstasy as it soars to freedom. This power, this life, is here calling you forward. Your consciousness is the passport to the beyond—the passport to the universe.

You have done the work, you have the ticket, and you have the passport, With this passport you are free to travel beyond any of the limitations you have imposed upon yourself in this life, and even beyond this confining idea that your life can ever really end. Soar beyond those doubts, soar beyond those limiting ideas, and find joy and peace in knowing that your flight is always able to open up to new vistas and unspeakably beautiful panoramas for your pleasure and fulfillment. Now is the time for you to be launched into those ever-greater heights of the splendor, wholeness and abundance that life offers. Fears cannot stand when you're going for life, for there's nothing to fear, not even death, when you are for life.

Rejoice in knowing and believing that this is the day of your spiritual takeoff. This is the day that you get to unfurl your wings and fly across the threshold to the beyond. I'll see you there!

LIFE
REVIEW
EXERCISE

Life Review Exercise

Below is a line divided into time segments, which you are asked to consider as representing your life. Use a large sheet of paper to reproduce this line as the beginning of this exercise:

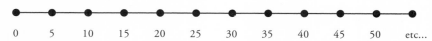

For each decision you made about something important in your life, put a dot. From that dot, draw a slanted line upward. On that slanted line, write the decision that you made. For example:

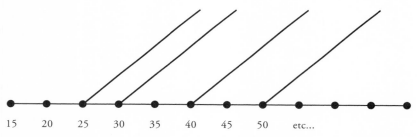

Now, to dramatize for yourself the force of that decision, from each dot draw a slanted dotted line downward, and write what might have happened if you hadn't made that decision, but rather its opposite. For example:

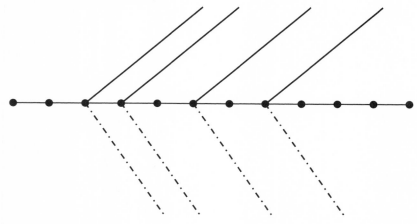

Life Review Exercise

Every dot on that line represents your freedom. This diagram is a reminder of how free you have been in your life–in other words, how often you had at least two things to choose between. Thus, it is a picture of the possible changes in your life.

It is also a picture of the common thread in your life–the common denominators and the constant values that ran through all of your decisions. Some of these common denominators may strike you instantly. Others may become clear to you only after some examination of the illustration, and your contemplation upon it.

Here are some questions that may help your contemplation. As you answer the questions involving other people, think of your family, classmates, playmates, colleagues, bosses, lovers, idols, rivals, teachers, etc.

What moments on the Life Review line stand out in sharpest detail in your memory?

Which faces from your past can you see most clearly?

Which voices can you hear most vividly?

Which of these did you trust the most?

Which of these did you most want to be like?

Which events moved you most deeply?

Which experiences molded or affected you the most?

Life Review Exercise (continued)

What were the scenes of your greatest sadness?

What were the scenes of your greatest joys?

What helped to preserve constancy in your life (for example: people, lack of geographical movement, few deaths, your memory, religion, isolation, etc.)?

What helped to bring about change in your life (for example: need for adventure, risk-taking, geographical movement, societal change, divorce, changing faiths, deaths, aging, etc.)?

What decision that you made do you regret the most?

SOAR

Spiritual Guidance for Overcoming Life's Turbulence

by Rev. Christian Sørenson D.D.

The text of this book was set in
11.5-point Adobe Garamond,
a typeface based on the sixteenth-century typedesigns of
Claude Garamond.

First Edition
Published November 2004

ABOUT THE AUTHOR

Rev. Christian Sorensen D.D. is the spiritual leader of Seaside Church, one of the fastest-growing churches in Encinitas California. He is also a past President and Community Leader of the United Church of Religious Science. Known as one of the most colorful and dynamic speakers in his field, he continues to thrill listeners with impassioned talks. He also serves on the Leadership Council of the Association of Global New Thought. He is a world traveler, leading groups to Tibet, India, China, Europe, Australia and New Zealand, and an avid sportsman whose love for surfing and skiing is legendary.